Rebel Recipes

niki webster

Rebel Recipes

maximum flavour, minimum fuss

niki webster

photography by
Kris Kirkham

BLOOMSBURY ABSOLUTE
LONDON · OXFORD · NEW YORK · NEW DELHI · SYDNEY

believe in the **MAGIC**
of **your dreams**

For all the readers of
Rebel Recipes, my family
and friends.

Much love, Niki x

contents

Introduction   8   Here It is... 10
                          Where It All Began 12
                          Store Cupboard Essentials 14

RISE UP TO *rule-breaking* **BREAKFASTS**   20   Quick and Easy 22
                          Transformative Toast Toppers 32
                          Brunch 42
                          Big Vegan Breakfasts 53
                          Curry for Breakfast 58

Rebelicious **MAINS**   68   Radical Curries and Delectable Dals 70
                          World Flavours 88
                          Comfort Food 108
                          Incredible Pastas and Risottos 128

small **PLATES,** **SOUPS** *and* **SALADS**   140   Small Plates 143
                          A Soup for All Seasons 162
                          Salad Bliss 173

AGAINST *the* **GRAIN**   186   Flatbreads and Pizzas 189
                          Life-changing Pancake Breads 195

Can't Believe It's Vegan **DESSERTS**   202   Pure Comfort 206
                          Something Special 215
                          Tempting Tarts 226
                          A Little Lighter 234

THE REBEL **PANTRY**   242   Devilish Dips and Sauces 244
                          Life-changing Dressings 258
                          Pickle and Preserve Like a Pro 261
                          Plant-based Milks 268
                          Nut Butters 270

the END   272   Index 274
                          About the Author 280
                          Acknowledgements 283

Introduction

Here It Is... 10 Where It All Began 12 Store Cupboard Essentials 14 Quick and Easy Transformative Toast Toppers Brunch Big Vegan Breakfasts Curry for Breakfast Radical Curries and Delectable Dals World Flavours Comfort Food Incredible Pastas and Risottos Small Plates A Soup for All Seasons Salad Bliss Flatbreads and Pizzas Life-changing Pancake Breads Pure Comfort Something Special Tempting Tarts A Little Lighter Devilish Dips and Sauces Life-changing Dressings Pickle and Preserve Like a Pro Plant-based Milks Nut Butters Index About the Author Acknowledgements Here It Is... Where It All Began Store Cupboard Essentials Quick and Easy Transformative Toast Toppers Brunch Big Vegan Breakfasts Curry for Breakfast Radical Curries and Delectable Dals World Flavours Comfort Food Incredible Pastas and Risottos Small Plates A Soup for All Seasons Salad Bliss Flatbreads and Pizzas Life-changing Pancake Breads Pure Comfort Something Special Tempting Tarts A Little Lighter Devilish Dips and Sauces Life-changing Dressings Pickle and Preserve Like a Pro Plant-based Milks Nut Butters Index About the Author Acknowledgements Here It Is... Where It All Began Store Cupboard Essentials Quick and Easy Transformative Toast Toppers Brunch Big Vegan Breakfasts Curry for Breakfast Radical Curries and Delectable Dals World Flavours Comfort Food Incredible Pastas and Risottos Small Plates A Soup for All Seasons Salad Bliss Flatbreads and Pizzas Life-changing Pancake Breads Pure Comfort Something Special Tempting Tarts A Little Lighter Devilish Dips and Sauces Life-changing Dressings Pickle and

Here it is,
my *Rebel Recipes* book
– *a book for* plant-loving rebels!

This book and my recipes are a celebration of vegetables, their vibrancy, flavours and colours; they are at the heart of all my dishes, and I build recipes around them. I believe that plant-based food doesn't need to be ordinary, you just need a little creativity and your meals can be bursting with unexpected flavour while still being healthy and uncomplicated. For me, eating is all about pleasure – food that will feed your soul as well as your belly.

The food within these pages is the food I love to eat: delicious, wholesome plant-based dishes which aren't too complicated to make and will help you create tasty feasts without too much fuss. My recipes are unashamedly about taste whilst being intrinsically balanced and healthy.

All my recipes are vegan, and most are naturally gluten free (although I've included some wheat where I feel the recipe needs it) but all are full of taste. You won't find any limp lettuce or boring old school bland veggie burgers, tasteless tofu or 'fake' food here, just great-tasting wholesome deliciousness. My hope is that everyone from vegans and vegetarians through to people just wanting to reduce their meat consumption will find something they love within this book.

Many of the recipes have been inspired by my travels and the world flavours and plant-centric cuisines that I've been lucky enough to encounter, often using spices, herbs and slow cooking to maximise the flavour of the vegetables and pulses, layering textures and flavours to build truly magnificent meals. Lots of my recipes reflect this, so be prepared for spicy curries, lots of pulses, flatbreads, salad, dips and pickles. It is food to be shared and enjoyed. Soul food.

I love a curry for breakfast. Having spent many months in India enjoying gorgeously spiced dosas and idlis, I'll be forever hooked. But I've also enjoyed huge salads with dips and pittas in Israel for breakfast, or rice soup in Thailand, so I know breakfasts around the world don't necessarily rely on sweet or processed foods as they can do in the west. And as a breakfast obsessive, I'd like to challenge the rules of what should and shouldn't be eaten for certain meals a little here. So, you'll find lots of rule-breaking recipes, including curry for breakfast!

My aim is that each chapter demonstrates how to bring taste, spice and innovative ways to make your day burst with deliciousness and health, showing just how varied a plant-based diet can be. As I naturally steer towards comfort foods, you can expect to find big bowls of soup, curries, dals and bakes, alongside fresh salads, brunch ideas and, of course, decadent desserts.

I've included some of my old favourite recipes, the ones I've been making for years that have been tried, tested and loved by my family, friends and blog readers (with some little tweaks here and there) and plenty of new ones I can't wait for you to try.

Niki Webster x
Birmingham, 2019

Where *it* all began

For me plant-based eating isn't just a trend – 'meat and two veg' have always been off the agenda, much to my mum's dismay, as I pretty much refused to eat meat from a young age. I was labelled a picky eater (throw in a dairy intolerance as well) but as soon as I could get into the kitchen as a teenager I started to experiment to try and create the food I wanted to eat. Back then it was mostly adding curry paste to veggies, but I loved it.

Through lots of trial and error I was soon making the food I loved and I've continued to experiment ever since. Back then there wasn't the explosion of vegan and vegetarian options there are now, so I had to be super creative with the limited ingredients available. It was at about the same time that my interest in travelling started in earnest and I discovered the delights of Asian and Middle Eastern cuisine which I tried to recreate whenever I was home.

Not surprisingly, after university I chose a career in food marketing and social media, which I loved and continued in until I decided it was time to follow my passion for food full time. However, I've been lucky in that I've always managed to squeeze in lots of time travelling: Europe, Africa and six months backpacking around Asia, trying the amazing local food. I just love Indian thalis and dosas, Thai flavours, Middle Eastern food and huge mezzes with hummus and flatbread – there's so much to explore and enjoy!

When I launched my blog, Rebel Recipes, in 2015 it was just a place to share my recipes and foodie passion. I had no idea where it would take me, and it's pretty amazing that this has become my full-time job and is now a book – I couldn't be more happy and grateful. And I'm still travelling as much as possible and discovering new flavours and techniques which I now share with my followers.

The question I get asked all the time is 'why did you call your blog Rebel Recipes?' The simple answer is that when it started it was all about non-conformity. Unfortunately, there are sometimes unwritten rules that dictate the way we eat, and these tend to imply that all indulgent food is bad for you and all healthy food (especially plant-based) must be boring. As a passionate vegan foodie, I have always refused to accept this status quo. My food is unashamedly for foodies; it's about the pleasure of creating and eating great-tasting food. For me cooking is about challenging convention and rebelling against the rules in a fun way, creating accessible, inventive and delicious recipe ideas.

Incredibly after only a year of blogging I won the Soil Association BOOM Award for Best Organic Food Blog – a cause I'm super passionate about. My blog has also given me the opportunity to travel further, and to some amazing places like the Caribbean and Bali, to India to style for an incredible Ayurvedic cookbook, to Israel for a vegan food tour, and to Barcelona for cooking retreats – all fuelling my inspiration further.

Eating WHOLEFOODS, SEASONAL *and* ORGANIC

My approach to health and nutrition has evolved over the years and I believe that there isn't really a one-size-fits-all approach to a healthy diet. And, of course, it's not just food which plays a role in your wellbeing. I therefore stick (mostly) to a simple principle: eating natural wholefoods that are minimally processed. Real food. I also love to eat seasonally wherever possible. That means that vegetables and fruit are not only at their best, they should also be cheaper.

It's hard to believe now but for many years I had a very restrictive diet. I imposed lots of rules about what I should and shouldn't be eating. It's interesting because as soon as I relaxed my so called 'healthy' diet the digestive issues which I'd struggled with for years hugely improved.

From my personal experience eating a more varied and abundant plant-based diet full of wholefoods and incorporating more fermented foods has transformed my digestion.

As good gut health is linked to overall physical and mental health, I definitely think it's worth taking care of those good bacteria. You'll therefore find some recipes for kimchi and sauerkraut in this book – I like to eat them with salads, curries, on toast. Everything.

And whenever possible I try to eat organic; I think eating produce which has been grown using fewer pesticides, no preservatives or GM is completely sensible. Not to mention the benefits for wildlife and the environment. I find investing in a seasonal organic veg box is a brilliant way to get your fruit and veg. It does sometimes mean you need to be a bit more creative, but it's cost effective and you know what you're eating. And it tastes great!!

Store cupboard *essentials* –
THE REBEL **PANTRY**

A well-stocked pantry (or cupboard) means that you should have everything you need to make a delicious meal quickly, and often you just need to add some fresh veg. At the back of the book I've given recipes for my dips, sauces, pickles, nut butters and plant-based milks, but below is a pretty comprehensive list of store cupboard essentials that you'll find in my kitchen. You definitely don't need all of them, but I hope it will help you navigate my recipes more easily.

SPICES

These are essential for adding flavour, so I like to keep a fully stocked spice drawer; here are some of my favourite combinations:

African: *Berbere blend, harissa blend, fenugreek*
General: *garlic powder*
Heat: *chilli flakes, hot paprika, cayenne*
Indian spices: *cumin seeds, cinnamon, black mustard seeds, curry leaves, turmeric, coriander, garam masala*
Middle Eastern: *fennel, caraway, zaatar*
Smokey flavours: *smoked paprika, ancho chilli, sweet paprika*
Sweet: *cinnamon, ginger, all spice, mixed spice, cloves, nutmeg*
Thai: *lemongrass, kaffir lime leaves, galangal, chilli*

Fresh HERBS

Many of my recipes, both sweet and savoury, contain fresh herbs. They pack a flavour punch and can transform your meal in minutes. My favourites, and the ones I tend to have a stock of, are thyme, mint, coriander and basil (essential for making huge batches of pesto). (While it's not a herb, spinach is certainly the most versatile leaf and I add it to salads, curries, stews and pestos.)

NUTS *and* **SEEDS**

These morsels of goodness add crunch, texture, protein and good fats. I like to add a little to most meals and this is my top tip for feeling satisfied.

Seeds: *dry toast them to elevate the flavour*
Nuts: *you only need to use them sparingly to add lots of texture and flavour*
Nut butters: *I usually have at least two or three types of nut butter on the go. They are perfect for dolloping into oats, spreading on toast, making dressings and generally adding lots of healthy fats to a meal in minutes*
Tahini: *one of my favourite ingredients, it is delicious used in desserts, and tahini dressing is amazing*

Oils

I feel like oils have a bad reputation. Yes, they are high in calories, but they add so much flavour and a little goes a long way.

Olive oil: *I mostly use olive oil for cooking and roasting*
Extra virgin olive oil: *adds delicious flavour for dressing, dips and pestos*
Rapeseed oil: *contains less saturated fat than other cooking oils. High in omega 3, 6 and 9. Use for roasting and stir fries as it has a higher smoking point than olive oil. Delicious!*
Toasted sesame oil: *essential for adding that toasted flavour to Asian dishes*
Coconut oil: *I tend to use this only for Asian food (and as a brilliant moisturiser)*

COCONUT **PRODUCTS**

Coconut is a dream ingredient; it adds a huge amount of texture, flavour and creaminess to vegan food, and a little goes a long way!

Coconut yogurt: *add a few tablespoons to curries, soups, stews for a rich creamy texture and flavour*
Coconut cream: *the key to deliciously creamy desserts*
Coconut milk: *for creamy curries, rice and desserts*

Egg REPLACERS

There are so many good solutions for replacing eggs in vegan baking – here are my top suggestions:

Chia or flax egg: *mix 1 tablespoon of flax/chia with 2 tablespoons of water per egg*
Aquafaba: *use 3 tablespoons per egg*
Banana: *I use mashed banana as a brilliant binder and sweetener in desserts*
Avocado, chestnuts or tofu: *all add moisture and bind well*
Peanut butter: *use 3 tablespoons per egg. Perfect for brownies*
Baking soda and vinegar: *use 1 tablespoon of apple cider vinegar and 1 teaspoon of baking soda to replace 1 egg. Best for cakes*

NATURAL *sweeteners*

Lots of vegan recipes still use refined sugars. I prefer natural replacements – yes they are still sugar but at least you are also gaining some nutrients.

Ripe bananas: *one of the best natural sweeteners around. Use in bakes, flapjacks and, of course, banana ice cream!*

Maple syrup: *my favourite liquid sweetener*

Coconut sugar: *Coconut palm sugar adds lots of lovely caramel flavours, lower in GI than cane sugar*

Cinnamon: *adds sweetness and flavour*

Dried fruits: *the must-have medjool date, plus figs, sultanas and apricots are great sweeteners*

Frozen fruit: *I always have plenty in my freezer. Freeze batches in the summer so you can enjoy throughout the year in porridges and smoothies, or for compotes and chia jam. Particular favourites are blueberries, blackberries, raspberries and cherries*

CONDIMENTS

My fridge is packed with condiments (so much so, I have serious top shelf bend!). Here are my go-tos:

Apple cider vinegar: *give a gut-loving kick to dressings and sauces. Anti-bacterial and anti-inflammatory, I recommend getting one with a mother.*

Mustards: *Dijon and wholegrain are my favourites*

Tamari: *gluten-free soy. Essential!*

Miso: *use brown rice for Asian dishes or white miso for a sweeter flavour*

Sriracha: *I'm never without this; it's great for pimping meals in seconds*

Gochujang: *a fermented red chilli paste, essential for Korean dishes*

Rose harissa: *another obsession of mine, it adds incredible depth of flavour and colour, and is more subtle than harissa paste*

Mirin: *sweet Japanese cooking wine*

Balsamic: *both vinegar and glaze are important condiments in my kitchen*

Tamarind paste: *one of my favourite Indian flavours*

Nutritional yeast: *the magic ingredient for anything nutty, cheesy or creamy. It makes the perfect cheese sauce (with cashews). Add to pestos or other sauces. Great source of B vitamins. (It's deactivated yeast by the way.)*

MILKS

There are some brilliant plant-based milks in shops now. It's also easy to make your own so I've provided some recipes in the pantry chapter. Listed here are my top choices for pairings:

Almond: *perfect for adding to your oats and in baking*

Cashew: *delicious in hot chocolate, turmeric lattes and of course curries*

Coconut: *great for most things but I love in; Asian dishes, porridge, matcha lattes and baking*

Hazelnut: *gorgeous in coffee*

Oat: *very versatile but particularly good in lattes and overnight oats*

Seasoning

I think people can be a bit fearful of seasoning; however it's essential for flavour. If you're not eating a highly processed diet (which tends to be packed full of unhealthy salt) you don't need to be afraid of adding quality salt to dishes. The following are my go-to seasonings:

Sea salt flakes

Pink Himalayan salt

Black pepper

Lemon juice: *immediately enhances flavour, a squeeze of lemon can go a long way*

Seaweed: *a real super superfood, it is absolutely packed with nutrients, high in fibre and protein. Adds lots of savoury seasoning*

Stock: *I absolutely love Marigold Bouillon and it works brilliantly in soups, stews and for the perfect 'cheeseless' cheese sauce*

FLOURS

I honestly can't live without a variety of flours; I use multiple types every day. It's also good to mix different gluten-free flours to improve the texture and flavour. Below is a list of some that you'll commonly see in my recipes, and that I always have a stash of at home:

Buckwheat: *my favourite and I love to use it for flatbreads and desserts as it has a slightly nutty flavour. It's actually a seed not a grain and naturally gluten free*

Gram: *a firm favourite with great protein content, it is gluten free and makes amazing crepes and vegan 'omelettes'*

Teff: *a tiny ancient grain originating from Ethiopia, it makes the amazing injera bread*

Rice: *brilliant in desserts and in a mix of gluten-free flours*

Rye and spelt: *I love using these ancient grains for delicious flatbreads and loaves; both provide a lovely nutty texture*

Semolina/rava: *great for making delicious dosas*

Good-quality plain flour: *nothing matches the results of good old plain flour if you want a fluffy flatbread or pizza base*

Oat: *simply blitz oats to a fine flour and use for tart crusts or desserts*

PULSES *and* RICE

I try to include pulses in most of my meals. They are satisfying, delicious and packed full of protein. If you're concerned about getting enough protein in your diet you can easily create completely plant-based protein by combining legumes and wholegrains, for example rice with beans, peanut butter or hummus on toast, dal with flatbread – the list goes on. These are the pulses I always have in stock:

Chickpeas: *I tend to have a combination of dried chickpeas which I cook in batches and freeze in hummus-size portions and also use organic canned. I save the aquafaba (bean water) for use later*

Red split lentils: *I have a massive jar full of these. You can make a delicious dal in 15 minutes.*

Puy lentils: *the earthy flavour and texture is amazing, a very 'meaty' lentil*

Quinoa: *a tasty and healthy alternative to pasta or rice, there are now some amazing British producers of quinoa*

Channa dal: *brilliant for dals and curries*

Frozen peas: *a favourite ingredient of mine! You can make an amazing dip/ mash in minutes, and they add fantastic plant-based protein to curries*

Tofu: *I always have both firm and silken at home. I tend to pan fry firm with spices until beautifully crispy on the outside and soft inside, and silken is perfect for desserts and vegan 'omelettes'.*

Rice: *arborio (for risottos), wild (big rice salads), black (with bold Asian flavours), basmati (with curries) – I love them all*

RISE UP TO
rule-breaking
BREAKFASTS

Here It Is... Where It All Began Store Cupboard Essentials **Quick and Easy 22 Transformative Toast Toppers 32 Brunch 42 Big Vegan Breakfasts 53 Curry for Breakfast 58** Radical Curries and Delectable Dals World Flavours Comfort Food Incredible Pastas and Risottos Small Plates A Soup for All Seasons Salad Bliss Flatbreads and Pizzas Life-changing Pancake Breads Pure Comfort Something Special Tempting Tarts A Little Lighter Devilish Dips and Sauces Life-changing Dressings Pickle and Preserve Like a Pro Plant-based Milks Nut Butters Index About the Author Acknowledgements Here It Is... Where It All Began Store Cupboard Essentials Quick and Easy Transformative Toast Toppers Brunch Big Vegan Breakfasts Curry for Breakfast Radical Curries and Delectable Dals World Flavours Comfort Food Incredible Pastas and Risottos Small Plates A Soup for All Seasons Salad Bliss Flatbreads and Pizzas Life-changing Pancake Breads Pure Comfort Something Special Tempting Tarts A Little Lighter Devilish Dips and Sauces Life-changing Dressings Pickle and Preserve Like a Pro Plant-based Milks Nut Butters Index About the Author Acknowledgements Here It Is... Where It All Began Store Cupboard Essentials Quick and Easy Transformative Toast Toppers Brunch Big Vegan Breakfasts Curry for Breakfast Radical Curries and Delectable Dals World Flavours Comfort Food Incredible Pastas and Risottos Small Plates A Soup for All Seasons Salad Bliss Flatbreads and Pizzas Life-changing Pancake Breads Pure Comfort Something Special Tempting Tarts A Little Lighter Devilish Dips and Sauces Life-changing

There's nothing quite like the flavour combination of cherries and almonds. My mum would occasionally treat my sister and me to a Mr Kipling Bakewell and I think that's where my obsession started. These parfaits remind me of that favourite childhood dessert, but with layers of creamy chia and oats, sweet seasonal cherries, vanilla coconut yoghurt and some almond butter for good measure. It's perfect as a luxurious breakfast or a healthy dessert.

Cherry Bakewell chia parfaits

Makes 2 large portions or 4 small

For the chia and oat layer

1 tablespoon chia seeds
4 tablespoons jumbo oats
4 tablespoons chopped hazelnuts
2 tablespoons ground almonds
250ml almond milk or plant-based milk of choice
1 teaspoon almond extract
½ teaspoon vanilla extract
1 teaspoon maple syrup

For the cherry layer

180g fresh cherries, pitted, or frozen cherries, defrosted
1 tablespoon maple syrup or sweetener of choice
¼ teaspoon vanilla extract

For the coconut layer

125g coconut yoghurt
1 teaspoon maple syrup, optional
½ teaspoon vanilla extract

To serve

2 tablespoons toasted flaked almonds
a handful of fresh cherries
fresh mint leaves

Firstly, put all the ingredients for the chia and oat layer in a jar. Mix to combine well. Pop it in the fridge overnight so that the chia and oats swell.

To prepare the cherry layer, put the cherries in a small frying pan with the maple syrup, vanilla and a splash of water. Cook over a medium heat for a few minutes until the cherries soften a little. Set aside.

For the coconut layer, combine the ingredients in a small bowl.

To assemble, give the chia and oat mix a quick stir, adding a little more milk if needed, then divide between two medium-sized or four small pots. Next, add some cherries followed by the coconut yoghurt. Repeat the layering until done. Top with the flaked almonds, extra cherries and fresh mint and serve.

Did you know that traditionally Scottish porridge was made with just oats, salt and water and stirred with a spurtle (a wooden kitchen tool)? That aside, there's nothing quite like a warm bowl of porridge to wrap your hands around and warm your insides on a cold winter morning. These creamy coconutty oats simmered in spices and then topped with crispy caramelised banana are pretty special.

Creamy spiced coconut porridge *with* sticky sesame banana

Serves 1

50g jumbo oats

250ml plant-based milk of choice, plus extra if needed

1 teaspoon ground ginger

½ teaspoon ground turmeric

½ teaspoon ground cinnamon

1 teaspoon vanilla extract

¼ teaspoon ground cardamom

2 tablespoons coconut yoghurt

1 teaspoon maple syrup, optional

freshly ground black pepper

For the sticky sesame banana

1 tablespoon toasted sesame oil

1 tablespoon maple syrup

1 banana, peeled and sliced lengthways

2 tablespoons sesame seeds

First, make the sticky sesame banana. Heat a non-stick frying pan over a medium heat. Pour in the sesame oil and maple syrup and swirl around the pan.

Next, add the sliced banana, and fry on the one side for a few minutes, until starting to caramelise. Flip and repeat on the other side. Turn off the heat and sprinkle with the sesame seeds. Carefully flip again to coat the banana pieces all over with the seeds.

To make the porridge, add the oats, milk and spices to a small saucepan and place over a low heat. Bring to a simmer and stir continuously, for a few minutes, until the porridge has absorbed the milk but is not too dry. Turn off the heat and stir in the coconut yoghurt and, if using, the maple syrup. Add a splash more milk if needed.

Spoon into a bowl and top with the banana and a small pinch of pepper.

Nutty tahini overnight oats *with* warm blackberries

These little pots of gooey oats changed my breakfasts forever, and are now a staple in my house.

Try stirring tahini into the oats for a delicious and nutritious change from nut butter – the lovely contrast of cold creamy oats and warm sticky berries is just delightful.

There are so many flavour options but some of my favourite combinations are peanut butter and banana; apple and cinnamon; and fresh berries and dates. In fact the toppings make all the difference – elevating tasty oats to incredible oats.

Serves 1

3–4 tablespoons jumbo oats
   or oats of choice
1 tablespoon tahini
1 tablespoon coconut yoghurt
2 tablespoons chopped
   hazelnuts
½ teaspoon vanilla extract
plant-based milk of choice,
   to cover
1 teaspoon sweetener of choice
   (maple syrup, rice malt syrup
   or agave syrup), if needed

For the blackberry compote

2 handfuls of blackberries
1 teaspoon maple syrup

For the optional toppings

cacao nibs
fresh thyme or mint leaves

Firstly, add the oats, tahini, yoghurt, nuts and vanilla extract to a Mason jar or a bowl, and mix to combine.

Add enough milk to completely cover the oats. Cover and soak overnight in the fridge.

The next day, make the compote by putting the blackberries, maple syrup and a splash of water in a small saucepan. Place over a medium heat until the berries start to melt down a little.

Add a little sweetener and more milk to the oats, if needed, to loosen the mixture.

Transfer the oats to a bowl, top with the compote and add one or more of the optional toppings as desired.

During my first visit to India, many years ago, I fell in love with the savoury and sweet lassi. Lassis were always refreshing no matter how hot the day was. I wanted to take that inspiration and make the drink my own.

This recipe blends coconut yoghurt with mango and lots of subtle spices and is absolutely gorgeous. I would also recommend trying the variation below for the most delicious breakfast.

Coconut *and* mango lassi

Serves 2

For the lassi

125ml coconut yoghurt
125ml coconut milk or plant-based milk of choice
½ medium ripe mango
1 large ripe frozen banana
½ teaspoon ground turmeric
¼ teaspoon ground cardamom
¼ teaspoon ground cinnamon
¼ teaspoon vanilla extract
a thumb-sized piece of ginger, finely grated
1 tablespoon maple syrup

For the topping

2 tablespoons coconut flakes
1 tablespoon sesame or sunflower seeds
cacao nibs
½ ripe mango, peeled and destoned

Firstly, toast the coconut flakes and seeds for the topping in a small frying pan until lightly golden brown. Set aside.

Add the lassi ingredients to a high-speed blender or food processor and blitz until very creamy. Divide between two glasses, top with the toasted coconut flakes and seeds, the cacao nibs and mango, and eat immediately.

variation

Put 6 tablespoons oats in a bowl and stir through the lassi. Divide between two jars, close the lid and refrigerate overnight. You may want to loosen the mixture by adding some more plant-based milk. Top with a few chunks of mango to serve if you like.

At one of my favourite restaurants in Barcelona, Flax & Kale, they serve a healthy mochaccino – I'm obsessed with it and have to have one whenever I'm in Barcelona. It has inspired me to create these healthier choc pots made from frozen bananas, raw cacao, peanut butter and a shot of espresso. They might just be the ultimate breakfast pick me up.

Peanut butter *and* choc frappé pots

Serves 2

2 medium ripe frozen bananas
a double shot of espresso
    (around 55ml), cooled
2 tablespoons coconut
    yoghurt or plant-based
    yoghurt of choice
1 tablespoon raw cacao powder
1 teaspoon vanilla extract
1 tablespoon peanut butter
2 teaspoons maple syrup or
    sweetener of choice
a pinch of sea salt flakes

For the optional toppings
coconut yoghurt
cacao nibs
chopped hazelnuts

Add the bananas to a food processor or high-speed blender with the other ingredients. Blend until smooth and creamy.

Divide between two glasses, and serve with any additional toppings.

Beans on toast is my ultimate comfort food, and the first thing I make when I get home after travelling. Even as a teenager I was spice obsessed and would flavour my beans with all sorts, but these are definitely a step up: homemade, deliciously spiced beans piled on to freshly toasted sourdough. They are also brilliant served with rice and a big crunchy slaw.

Masala beans *on* **toast**

Serves 4

4 chunky slices of sourdough or
    bread of your choice, toasted
a drizzle of extra virgin olive oil
fresh coriander, to serve

For the masala beans

1 tablespoon olive oil
a bunch of spring onions, sliced
3 garlic cloves, sliced
1 teaspoon cumin seeds
1 teaspoon fennel seeds
½ teaspoon ground turmeric
½ teaspoon garam masala
1 teaspoon smoked paprika
20 cherry tomatoes, chopped
    in half
1 tablespoon tomato purée
1 tablespoon rose harissa or
    1 teaspoon harissa paste
400g can of chickpeas, rinsed
    and drained
400g can of haricot beans,
    rinsed and drained
a pinch of dried chilli flakes
1 teaspoon maple syrup
1 teaspoon tamari
sea salt flakes and freshly
    ground black pepper

Add the olive oil and spring onions to a wide-bottomed pan and fry gently over a low heat for 3–5 minutes, until soft and browning. Add the garlic and spices and fry for 30 seconds more. Next, add the tomatoes, tomato purée, harissa and 175ml of water to the pan. Bring to the boil over a high heat, then reduce the heat to low and simmer for 10 minutes until slightly reduced.

Add the drained beans, chilli, maple syrup and tamari. Season with salt and pepper, and stir well. Simmer for a further 5 minutes.

Drizzle the toast with extra virgin olive oil, then top with the masala beans and a sprinkle of coriander.

You might think this is just a recipe for avocado on toast but once you start adding flavours and textures you have the ultimate breakfast or lunch that just keeps giving.

My version has a creamy butter bean and thyme hummus, spread with some harissa for smoky heat which is then topped with avocado, fresh thyme and chilli. But there are so many more delicious toppings: baked mushrooms give the meal a really delicious texture, scrambled tofu provides lots of plant-based protein, and masala beans (page 32) or roast tomatoes lend a real flavour contrast to the avocado.

Ultimate avocado *on* toast *with* butter bean *and* thyme hummus

Serves 2

4 slices sourdough bread
extra virgin olive oil, to drizzle
1 tablespoon rose harissa
1 large ripe avocado, destoned, peeled and sliced
1 thyme sprig, leaves picked
1 teaspoon black sesame seeds, optional
sea salt flakes and freshly ground black pepper

For the butter bean and thyme hummus

400g can of butter beans, rinsed and drained
2 garlic cloves, peeled
2 tablespoons coconut milk or yoghurt
1 tablespoon good-quality tahini
1 tablespoon extra virgin olive oil
1 teaspoon fresh thyme leaves

First make the hummus. Put the butter beans into a food processor or high-speed blender with the garlic, coconut milk, tahini and extra virgin olive oil. Blitz until smooth and creamy (about 2 minutes), then add a splash of water to loosen if needed. Season to taste with salt and pepper, add in the thyme leaves and blitz again.

Toast the bread. Arrange the toasts on two plates and drizzle with a little extra virgin olive oil. Top with a generous amount of the butter bean hummus, a dollop of harissa, the avocado slices, fresh thyme and, if using, the sesame seeds. Season with salt and pepper, and serve.

Loaded Kim-cheese *on* toast

Fermented foods have seen a big rise in popularity recently and for a very good reason. Not only are they delicious, adding layers of flavour to meals, but they're also great for supporting gut health with their plentiful good bacteria. As one with a bit of a sluggish digestive system, I like to eat fermented foods every day as I find that it really helps.

But what is kimchi cashew cheese I hear you say? It's a combination of creamy cashews, vegan kimchi, nutty sunflower seeds, tamari and tahini. Be warned, it's highly addictive.

Tip: the recipe for the kimchi cashew cheese makes enough for four servings. It will keep in the fridge for up to a week. Spread it on toast, jacket potatoes or even pizzas. Anything goes.

Serves 1

1 slice sourdough, toasted
½ ripe avocado, destoned
    and sliced
a sprinkle of black/white
    sesame seeds
a small handful of coriander,
    chopped, or cress

For the kimchi cashew
    cheese

200g cashews, soaked in water
    for at least 4 hours
2 tablespoons sunflower seeds
2 teaspoons tamari
4 teaspoons toasted sesame oil
2 tablespoons tahini
200g kimchi (page 262)
1 teaspoon maple syrup

Drain the cashews and add all the
ingredients for the kimchi cashew
cheese to a food processor or high-
speed blender and blitz until you
get a chunky paste.

Spread a generous amount of
the kimchi cashew cheese onto
the toast. Top with avocado,
sesame seeds and freshly
chopped coriander.

An admission here – yes, I was that student who crammed anything I could find in the cupboard between two slices of bread and into my faithful toastie machine. One such combo included this decadent trio of peanut butter, jam and banana. What a joy.

This is my idea of pure comfort – gooey sweet caramelised bananas, layered with peanut butter and a fresh raspberry compote all sandwiched in toasted bread (minus the toastie machine this time) and then dolloped with coconut tahini cream. It's deliciously indulgent and definitely good enough for dessert – or any time of day!

Peanut butter *and* caramelised banana toastie

Serves 1

2 slices sourdough or rye
   bread, toasted
2 tablespoons peanut butter

For the caramelised banana
1 teaspoon coconut oil
a splash of maple syrup
1 ripe banana, cut into slices

For the raspberry compote
100g raspberries
1 teaspoon maple syrup

For the coconut tahini cream
2 tablespoons coconut yoghurt
   or cream
1 teaspoon tahini
½ teaspoon vanilla extract

Start by caramelising the banana. Melt the coconut oil in a small frying pan over a medium-low heat. Add the maple syrup and swirl around the pan. Add the banana slices and fry until caramelised, then flip over to caramelise the other side. Set aside.

In a small saucepan, add the raspberries, maple syrup and a splash of water. Heat for 3 minutes, or until the berries start to break down a little. Set aside.

Mix all the ingredients for the coconut tahini cream in a small bowl.

To assemble the toastie, spread both slices of toast with peanut butter. Spoon the compote over one of the slices and then layer the caramelised banana on top. Spoon over the coconut tahini cream over the second piece of toast and then sandwich together so that everything is encased. Slice in half and devour!

This recipe has become a brunch favourite but is also an easy throw-together dinner served with a big salad. I am of course using the term 'frittata' loosely as there aren't any eggs involved, but I hope you'll agree that it's a similar principle. The 'eggy' part is made from a combination of silken tofu blended with gram (chickpea) flour, and the nutritional yeast flakes give it a cheesy flavour. Added to this are soft caramelised onions, cherry tomatoes and kale. The frittata is then topped with roast balsamic tomatoes and a generous drizzle of balsamic glaze. Absolutely delicious.

Caramelised onion *and* chickpea frittata *with* roast balsamic tomatoes

Serves 4

2 tablespoons olive oil
2 red onions, roughly chopped
3 garlic cloves, sliced
175g cherry tomatoes
100g kale (about 3 handfuls), tough
    stalks removed and torn
sea salt flakes and freshly ground
    black pepper

For the balsamic tomatoes
250g cherry tomatoes
½ teaspoon olive oil
a drizzle of balsamic glaze

For the frittata mix
250g soft silken tofu
½ teaspoon onion salt
1 teaspoon cumin seeds
½ teaspoon baking powder
120g gram (chickpea) flour
3 tablespoons nutritional
    yeast flakes
1 tablespoon apple cider vinegar
2 tablespoons fresh thyme leaves

To finish
1 thyme sprig, leaves picked
dried chilli flakes, optional
extra virgin olive oil
balsamic glaze

Preheat the oven to 180°C/160°C Fan/Gas Mark 4.

Prepare the balsamic tomatoes. Chop some of the tomatoes in half and add both the halved and whole tomatoes to a baking tray. Toss with the olive oil, balsamic glaze and a pinch of salt. Bake for 15–20 minutes until soft, splitting and slightly brown. Set aside.

Heat the oil in a large non-stick frying pan and fry the onions over a medium-low heat for about 15 minutes, until soft and caramelised. Add the garlic and fry for a minute further. Next, add the tomatoes and kale, allowing the kale to wilt and the tomatoes to soften and split a little. Stir in 1 teaspoon of salt and turn off the heat.

To make the frittata mix, put all the ingredients into a food processor or high-speed blender and add 175ml of water. Blitz until you have a smooth and creamy mix.

Pour the mix into the pan with the onions, kale and tomatoes. Spread out using a spatula if needed. Place the pan back over a low heat and cook for 7 minutes, until the frittata is nearly set.

Pop the frittata under a preheated grill for 2 minutes, until cooked through and starting to brown on top.

Top the frittata with the balsamic tomatoes, fresh thyme and, if using, the chilli flakes. Drizzle with extra virgin olive oil and balsamic glaze and season well with salt and pepper.

There's something special about these sweet crepes. Crepes can take a little effort to get right but they're always worth it once you bite into that fluffy sweetness. Here, I've used buckwheat flour to make them gluten free and added almond extract for its gorgeous flavour. Filled with peanut butter, cool and creamy coconut yoghurt and warm and gooey strawberries, they are crepe heaven.

Tip: do you find that your crepes stick to the pan? Make sure you wait until the bubbles appear on the surface of the crepe and the edges start to come away from the pan before you flip it. And a good-quality non-stick pan always helps.

Strawberry *and* peanut butter crepes

Makes enough for 2, approximately 6 crepes

80g buckwheat flour
½ teaspoon baking powder
1 tablespoon peanut butter
250ml almond milk or plant-
   based milk of choice
½ teaspoon almond extract
1 teaspoon maple syrup
½ teaspoon apple cider vinegar
rapeseed oil, for frying

For the strawberry compote

300g strawberries or berries
   of choice (I like blackberries
   or raspberries, too)
2 teaspoons maple syrup

For the filling

peanut butter
coconut yoghurt
fresh mint leaves

Add the flour and baking powder to a large bowl. Stir to combine. Add in the peanut butter, milk, almond extract, maple syrup and cider vinegar. Mix to form a smooth batter. Set aside for 15 minutes if you have time, or at least a couple of minutes.

Add a little oil to the base of a small non-stick frying pan. Add ⅓ cup of the batter to the pan and swirl it around to coat the base of the pan. Cook over a medium heat for approximately 2 minutes, until there are bubbles on the surface of the crepe and the edges come away from the pan, lifting up easily. Flip the crepe over and cook the other side for 30 seconds to a minute. Remove from the pan to a plate and cover with a clean tea towel to keep warm. Repeat the process with the rest of the batter.

Add the strawberries and maple syrup to a small saucepan and set over a medium heat. Let the berries break up a little, then remove from the heat.

Fill each crepe with some peanut butter, coconut yoghurt and about 1 tablespoon of the compote. Fold the crepe in half and then in half again, then serve with more compote, yoghurt and fresh mint.

Growing up in south Shropshire on the Welsh border we regularly went on camping or caravan holidays, and if my mum didn't make breakfast in the caravan as a treat we would go a café. My sister always used to choose Welsh rarebit with its oozing cheesy topping. It was her absolute favourite and still is to this day. So that's where the inspiration for this recipe came from. Imagine soft leeks and mushrooms melting into a cheesy sauce on top of chewy sourdough ... absolutely gorgeous.

'Cheesy' mushrooms *and* spinach *on* toast

Serves 2

1 tablespoon olive oil

75g leeks, trimmed and sliced into thin rings

250g small portobello mushrooms, sliced

2 handfuls of spinach (about 50g), roughly chopped

2 large slices or 4 small slices sourdough

1 thyme sprig, leaves picked

sea salt flakes and freshly ground black pepper

For the cheesy béchamel sauce

1 tablespoon vegan butter

2 tablespoons plain flour

250ml almond milk or plant-based milk of choice

2 tablespoons nutritional yeast flakes

Firstly, heat the olive oil in a frying pan over a medium heat. Add the leeks and cook for 4–5 minutes, until soft. Add the mushrooms, then fry for a further 4–5 minutes until soft. Season with salt and pepper and turn off the heat.

To make the cheesy béchamel sauce, melt the butter in a frying pan over a low heat then stir in the flour. Next, add the milk and nutritional yeast flakes. Simmer for 5 minutes, stirring constantly to ensure no lumps form. Now season well with salt and pepper, and remove from the heat.

Stir in the chopped spinach and half of the mushroom and leek mixture into the sauce. Remove from the heat; the spinach will wilt in the sauce.

Toast the bread slices on one side under the grill, then turn and top the other side of each slice with the cheesy mushroom mixture. Pop back under the grill for a few minutes, until the topping browns a little. Season with salt and pepper.

Serve topped with the remaining mushrooms and leeks and a scattering of fresh thyme.

I've spent a lot of time in France over the last ten years – regular holidays mixed with work trips – and I've found an abundance of food inspiration there. I particularly love the galettes, crepes made from buckwheat flour, a flour I now also use regularly to make flatbreads. I love buckwheat's earthy taste, its higher nutritional value compared to other flours and the fact that it's naturally gluten free.

I've added spinach to the crepe batter here but you can add in any herbs or leaves you want to create this lovely green colour. I then filled them with a rich and tangy caponata and a classic rich basil pesto. If you happen to have any leftover caponata I like to use it spread on toast or to top griddled aubergine. It's also delicious mixed into grains and leaves for a fantastic salad or served with more dips, good-quality olive oil and some flatbread. Yum!

Spinach crepes
with
caponata
and
basil pesto

Makes about 5

For the caponata

2 tablespoons olive oil

2 small aubergines, roughly chopped into cubes

1 red onion, finely sliced

1 teaspoon dried oregano

3 garlic cloves, finely sliced

4 tablespoons capers

75g green olives, pitted

3 tablespoons balsamic vinegar

10 cherry tomatoes, roughly chopped

1 teaspoon date syrup

a drizzle of extra virgin olive oil

30g toasted pine nuts

sea salt flakes and freshly ground black pepper

To make the caponata, heat the olive oil in a large pan, add in the aubergine and a pinch of salt. Cook for 5–6 minutes, over a medium heat, stirring occasionally. Lower the heat and add the onion and oregano. Cook for 3 minutes, then add the garlic and cook for a further minute. Add the capers, olives and balsamic vinegar, and cook for a couple of minutes. Stir through the tomatoes and date syrup, bring to a simmer and cook for about 15 minutes, or until all the vegetables are tender.

Season and add more vinegar to taste. Drizzle with a little extra virgin olive oil and scatter over the pine nuts.

For the crepes, combine the flour, spinach, garlic powder and salt in a large bowl. Add in the cider vinegar, extra virgin olive oil and 150ml of water. Mix to a smooth batter. Set aside for 10 minutes.

Meanwhile, make the pesto. Add the ingredients to a food processor or high-speed blender and blitz until everything is combined to your preferred texture, adding 1 tablespoon of water if necessary. (You may need to scrape the sides down a few times.) Set aside.

Heat a little oil in a small non-stick frying pan over a medium heat. Add ¼ cup of the batter to the pan and swirl around the bottom so you get an even

For the crepes

60g buckwheat flour
50g spinach, chopped very finely (ideally in a food processor)
½ teaspoon garlic powder
½ teaspoon sea salt flakes
1 teaspoon apple cider vinegar
1 tablespoon extra virgin olive oil
olive oil, for frying

For the basil pesto

2 tablespoons toasted pine nuts
30g basil
1 garlic clove, peeled
2 tablespoons nutritional yeast flakes
½ teaspoon sea salt flakes
2–3 tablespoons extra virgin olive oil

crepe. Cook for approximately 2 minutes, until there are bubbles on the surface of the crepe and the edges come away easily from the pan. Flip and cook on the other side for 30 seconds to a minute.

Remove from the pan, place on a plate and cover with a clean tea towel to keep warm. Repeat the process with the rest of the batter.

Serve the crepes either with the caponata and pesto spread on top or with the filling rolled inside.

variations

You can also create beautiful colourful crepes by adding grated beetroot or carrot instead of spinach. Here are a few of my other favourite toppings; muhammara and cashew cheese, beetroot dip hummus with hazelnut dukkah, kale pesto and slaw, hummus with ratatouille or just dipped into dal (page 70).

Big juicy baked (or fried) mushrooms always remind me of mushroom foraging when I was little girl in Shropshire. My sister and I loved hunting them out and afterwards my dad would fry them, filling the house with amazing mushroom smells.

Mine are topped with a delicious spinach and hazelnut pesto, and served with toasted sourdough and balsamic tomatoes. The tomatoes are an absolute must as they really bring out the flavour of the mushrooms and cut through their richness. This makes a great brunch or light lunch.

Baked mushrooms *with* spinach *and* hazelnut pesto

Serves 2

For the mushrooms

3 tablespoons extra virgin olive oil
2 garlic cloves, crushed
1 tablespoon balsamic vinegar
1 teaspoon Dijon mustard
4 portobello mushrooms, wiped clean using paper towels
sea salt flakes and freshly ground black pepper

For the balsamic tomatoes

2 tablespoons olive oil
a bunch of spring onions, finely sliced
4 garlic cloves, sliced
½ teaspoon caraway seeds
220g cherry tomatoes, sliced

Prepare the mushrooms. Put the extra virgin olive oil, garlic, balsamic vinegar and mustard. Season, replace the lid and shake to combine.

Pop the mushrooms into a large bowl or container and pour half the marinade over the top. Give them a stir and allow to marinate for at least 1 hour.

Preheat the oven to 180°C/160°C Fan/Gas Mark 4.

Arrange the mushrooms on a baking tray and spoon over the reserved marinade. Bake for 20 minutes.

Meanwhile, prepare the balsamic tomatoes. Heat the olive oil in a saucepan over a medium-low heat. Add the spring onions and fry for 2–3 minutes, until soft. Next, add the garlic and caraway seeds, and fry for a further minute. Now add the tomatoes, balsamic glaze and salt. Cook for 7–8 minutes, or until the tomatoes have softened. Taste and adjust the seasoning.

Make the pesto. Lightly toast the hazelnuts in a small dry frying pan until they turn a shade darker. Remove and allow to cool. Do the same with the pine nuts and allow to cool.

... ingredients and method continued on page 54

1 teaspoon balsamic glaze
½ teaspoon sea salt flakes

For the spinach and hazelnut pesto
50g hazelnuts
25g pine nuts
100g (about 3 handfuls) spinach
a handful of basil
juice of ½ lemon
½ teaspoon sea salt
2 garlic cloves, peeled
3 tablespoons nutritional
    yeast flakes
2 tablespoons extra virgin
    olive oil

To serve
4 slices sourdough
a drizzle of extra virgin olive oil
½ ripe avocado
fresh thyme sprigs or oregano,
    leaves picked

Put the hazelnuts and pine nuts in a food processor with 75ml of water and blitz with the remaining ingredients until everything is well mixed and you have your preferred texture. You may need to scrape down the sides a few times.

Toast the sourdough slices and drizzle with some extra virgin olive oil. Top with the pesto and baked mushrooms, then spoon over the balsamic tomatoes. Peel the avocado and remove the stone. Slice or dice and serve on top of the tomatoes. Sprinkle with the thyme or oregano leaves and serve immediately.

There are many versions of eggs baked in tomato sauce from cuisines all around the world – and they're all pretty genius. The first time I ate shakshuka – the Israeli version – was actually in Goa. I loved it, but have since created a few egg-free versions. This is definitely a vegan go-to dish, so if you've not tried it before I would highly recommend it.

My breakfast shakshuka has it all – a rich tomato sauce with roast veg, scrambled tofu, avocado and a big drizzle of tahini dressing. It's a breakfast feast that is perfect fare for lazy Sunday brunches with friends.

Big breakfast shakshuka

Serves 4

1 aubergine, sliced into 2.5cm rounds

4 tablespoons olive oil

1 teaspoon smoked garlic powder

2 red or orange peppers, deseeded and sliced lengthways

6 spring onions, roughly chopped

4 garlic cloves, sliced

1 teaspoon cumin seeds

6 tomatoes or 30 cherry tomatoes, roughly chopped

a pinch of dried chilli flakes

400g can of chickpeas, rinsed and drained

1-2 tablespoons coconut yoghurt, optional

sea salt flakes and freshly ground black pepper

For the quick tofu scramble

1 tablespoon olive oil

4 spring onions, sliced

Preheat the oven to 180°C/160°C Fan/Gas Mark 4.

Put the aubergine slices onto a roasting tray and coat in 2 tablespoons of the olive oil, the smoked garlic powder and a good grinding of pepper. Roast for about 40–45 minutes, turning occasionally. Set aside.

Chargrill the peppers on a griddle pan over a high heat for about 15 minutes, turning frequently until nice and charred on both sides. Set aside to cool, then peel away most of the charred skins and chop the flesh quite finely.

Heat the remaining 2 tablespoons of oil in a large frying pan and add the spring onions, garlic and cumin. Fry over a medium heat for 3–4 minutes, until the onions are just starting to colour and soften. Add the tomatoes and chilli flakes, and season with salt and pepper. Simmer for 15–20 minutes, until soft. (Note, you may need to top up with a little water if the mixture looks like it is getting too dry.)

Add the chickpeas and peppers to the pan, followed by half the aubergine slices and stir to combine. Simmer for a couple more minutes. If using, stir in the yoghurt.

Next, make the tofu scramble. Heat the olive oil in a small frying pan and add the spring onions. Fry for 3 minutes, until soft and browning. Add the tofu and the remaining ingredients, then mix everything to combine, breaking up the tofu a little.

... ingredients and method continued on page 56

400g packet of firm tofu, drained
and cut into small chunks
4 tablespoons nutritional
yeast flakes
2 teaspoons sea salt
2 teaspoons garlic powder
½ teaspoon ground turmeric
2 tablespoons vegan
Worcestershire sauce
2 teaspoons apple cider vinegar
2 tablespoons extra virgin olive oil

For the tahini coriander
dressing
juice of 1 lemon
a handful (about 15g) of
coriander leaves
1 tablespoon tahini

To serve
1 avocado, destoned and sliced
a handful of fresh coriander
1 spring onion, sliced
a pinch of caraway seeds

Add all the ingredients for the dressing to a mini food
processor along with 3–4 tablespoons of water and blitz until
creamy. Season to taste.

To serve, transfer the shakshuka to a large serving bowl and
dollop on the tofu scramble.

Top with avocado, the reserved roast aubergine, fresh
coriander, some spring onion and a drizzle of tahini dressing.
Sprinkle with the caraway seeds to finish.

Having spent many months backpacking the length and breadth of India, my boyfriend and I travelled in style on a Royal Enfield motorcycle piled up with us and our bags. Every day was a new culinary adventure as we stopped at villages along the way, and I now consider myself a bit of an Indian breakfast connoisseur. There's an incredible array of savoury spiced breakfast options but, for me, dosas and crepes with chutneys are pretty hard to beat.

My spiced gram (chickpea) flour crepes are very quick to make and perfect for dipping or scooping up chutneys, pickles and salad.

Here I've given two types of chutney – a quick coconut one and a sweet onion one. Both are perfect with these crepes, or with any of Indian-spiced curry or dal. The coconut chutney can be made in advance and will last at least a week in the fridge. The onion chutney can be made a couple of weeks in advance – the flavours will intensify but this step is not crucial.

Spiced crepes *with* coconut chutney *and* sweet onion chutney

Makes about 5

120g gram (chickpea) flour
½ teaspoon sea salt flakes
½ teaspoon garlic powder
½ teaspoon ground turmeric
½ teaspoon cumin seeds
½ teaspoon fennel seeds
½ teaspoon black
    mustard seeds
a pinch of dried chilli flakes
a handful of fresh coriander,
    plus extra to serve
a few curry leaves, optional
310ml lukewarm water
2 tablespoons olive oil

For the coconut chutney

50g unsweetened
    desiccated coconut
1 teaspoon grated ginger
½ small green chilli, deseeded
½ teaspoon sea salt flakes

To make the coconut chutney, add the desiccated coconut to a small bowl and cover with boiling water. Leave to rehydrate and soften, approximately 15 minutes.

Drain the softened coconut (reserving a few tablespoons of the soaking water) and add to a mini food processor or spice grinder with the ginger and chilli. Blend until smooth, adding some of the coconut soaking water to loosen if needed. Transfer to a bowl and stir through the salt and lime juice.

In a small frying pan over a medium-high heat, pour in the rapeseed oil. Once hot, add the mustard seeds and fry gently until the seeds start to pop. Immediately add in the cumin seeds and, if using, the curry leaves. Sauté for a few seconds. Tip the tempered spices and oil into the bowl with the coconut chutney and mix well. Set aside until required.

To make the onion chutney, heat the olive oil in a frying pan over a low heat. Add the onions, chilli, peppercorns and cumin seeds, and fry gently for about 20 minutes until the onions are dark brown and sticky. Add in the maple syrup and the balsamic vinegar and simmer for 30 minutes or so, until the chutney is thickened and darkened.

Pour the chutney into a sterilised jar if making in advance and allow to cool.

juice of ½ lime
2 teaspoons rapeseed or
    flaxseed oil
1 teaspoon black mustard seeds
½ teaspoon cumin seeds
6 curry leaves

For the sweet onion
  chutney

3 tablespoons olive oil
2 large onions, sliced into
    thin rings
½ teaspoon dried chilli flakes
1 teaspoon pink peppercorns
1 teaspoon cumin seeds
1½ tablespoons maple syrup
3 tablespoons balsamic vinegar

When you're ready to make the crepes, mix the dry ingredients in a large bowl. Add in the lukewarm water and olive oil, and whisk thoroughly until you get a thick batter. Stir in the coriander and curry leaves. Set aside for 15 minutes.

Heat a little oil in a small non-stick frying pan over a medium heat. Add ⅓ cup of the batter to the pan and swirl around the bottom so you get an even crepe. Cook for 1–2 minutes, until there are bubbles on the surface of the crepe and the edges come away slightly from the pan. Flip and cook on the other side for 30 seconds to a minute. Remove from the pan, place on a plate and cover with a clean tea towel to keep warm. Repeat the process with the rest of the batter.

Serve the crepe topped with the chutneys, and add a few coriander leaves. Roll up and eat straight away.

Not in the least bit traditional but if you love curry, and enjoy eating it for breakfast like me, then this is for you. The super speedy lightly spiced mushroom, spinach and bean stew gets scooped up with a quick and easy rye roti. Healthy, comforting and just downright tasty – double the recipe and you can eat it for dinner as well.

Breakfast curry *with* quick rye roti

Serves 2

2 tablespoons olive oil
1 teaspoon black mustard seeds
1 teaspoon cumin seeds
1 teaspoon ground coriander
½ teaspoon dried chilli flakes
1 teaspoon ground turmeric
1 onion, finely chopped
2 garlic cloves, sliced
400g cherry tomatoes, chopped
150g mushrooms, stalks
   removed, thinly sliced
2 handfuls (about 50g)
   of spinach
400g can of cannellini beans,
   rinsed and drained
fresh coriander, roughly
   chopped, to serve
sea salt flakes and freshly
   ground black pepper

For the quick rye roti
200g rye flour, plus extra
   to dust
1 teaspoon baking powder
100g coconut yoghurt

First, make the roti. Combine the flour, baking powder and a pinch of salt in a large bowl. Now add 75ml of water and the yoghurt, then mix thoroughly to combine.

Transfer the dough to a floured surface and knead for a few minutes until you have a smooth and springy dough. Pop the dough back in the bowl and leave to sit for 15 minutes.

To cook the curry, first add the olive oil to a large saucepan and set over a medium-low heat. Add in the spices. Once the seeds begin to pop, stir for a few seconds, then add the onion. Fry for 8–10 minutes, until soft and beginning to brown.

Now add in the garlic and stir for a few more minutes, then stir in the chopped tomatoes. Turn up the heat to medium, add 125ml of water followed by the mushrooms and cook for a further 7–8 minutes.

Finally, throw in the spinach and drained beans, and season well with salt and pepper. Stir to combine, allowing the spinach to wilt down.

Heat a large griddle pan or frying pan over a medium heat.

Divide the dough into four portions. Take one portion of dough, roll into a ball and place on a floured surface, then use a rolling pin to roll out your first roti – each disc should be about 2–3mm thick.

Pop the roti on the pan and allow to cook and char for 2–3 minutes, then flip and repeat on the other side. Remove and keep warm on a plate covered with a clean cloth. Repeat until all the rotis are done.

Serve the curry garnished with some chopped coriander and have the rotis on the side for scooping.

When I'm in India, it's impossible to resist all my favourite savoury breakfasts, but I am intrigued by the gorgeous sweet and delicately spiced options too.

This milk pudding is inspired by *kheer*, a sweet Indian dessert typically made with rice or vermicelli and condensed milk. It is absolutely delicious and I hope I've captured a little of the spirit here. My version of the pudding is made with oats, dates, banana and cardamom and I love it. Eat it straight away or chill in the fridge and wake up to the best overnight oats ever.

Date, oat *and* cardamom milk pudding

Serves 2

2 tablespoons almond butter
5 medjool dates, pitted,
   2 roughly chopped
50g jumbo oats
500ml coconut or almond milk
1 small banana, peeled
   and chopped
1 teaspoon ground cardamom
a handful of chopped hazelnuts,
   to serve (optional)

Firstly, blitz the almond butter with the 3 whole dates and 60ml of water in a food processor or high-speed blender to make a paste. Set aside.

Put the oats into a saucepan and toast over a medium-high heat, stirring continuously until you smell a nutty aroma – around 2–3 minutes. Next, add the milk, the almond-date paste, the remaining chopped dates and the banana to the pan. Bring to the boil, reduce the heat to low and cook for 15 minutes until thickened. Add the ground cardamom, stir to combine and remove the pan from the heat.

Serve immediately with some chopped hazelnuts.

variation

To make overnight oats, allow the pudding to cool and transfer to a jar. Seal with a lid and pop it in the fridge overnight. You might want to add a bit of milk when serving to loosen up the mix.

Caramelised shallots cooked with south Indian spices, garlic and ginger – it sounds basic but the flavours are to die for. Throw in potatoes, fry until crispy, then wilt in the spinach and you have a dish good enough for brunch, or dinner served with dal and a big slaw to add extra crunch.

Spiced potatoes
and spinach

Serves 4

400g potatoes, peeled and cut
    into 2.5cm dice
400g sweet potatoes, peeled
    and cut into 3cm dice
3 tablespoons olive oil
2 teaspoons cumin seeds
2 teaspoons black
    mustard seeds
4 echalion shallots, finely sliced
3 garlic cloves, crushed
a thumb-sized piece of ginger,
    peeled and finely chopped
1 teaspoon ground coriander
½ teaspoon ground turmeric
1 teaspoon garam masala
150ml vegetable stock
100g spinach leaves
a pinch of dried chilli flakes
juice of ¼ lemon
sea salt flakes

Bring a large pan of salted water to the boil, then add the potatoes. Simmer over a medium heat for 10 minutes until tender with a bit of bite. Drain and set aside.

Heat 2 tablespoons of the olive oil in a large frying pan and add the cumin and mustard seeds. Fry for 1–2 minutes, over a medium heat until the seeds begin to pop. Next, add in the shallots and fry until softened.

Add the garlic, ginger, coriander, turmeric and garam masala, and stir-fry for a further minute. Now add the boiled potatoes and the remaining tablespoon of oil. Reduce the heat to medium–low and fry for 5 minutes until slightly crispy.

Add the stock and stir in the spinach, allowing it to soften. Season with salt and chilli flakes, then squeeze over the lemon juice.

Rebelicious
MAINS

Here It Is... Where It All Began Store Cupboard Essentials Quick and Easy Transformative Toast Toppers Brunch Big Vegan Breakfasts Curry for Breakfast **Radical Curries and Delectable Dals 70 World Flavours 88 Comfort Food 108 Incredible Pastas and Risottos 128** Small Plates A Soup for All Seasons Salad Bliss Flatbreads and Pizzas Life-changing Pancake Breads Pure Comfort Something Special Tempting Tarts A Little Lighter Devilish Dips and Sauces Life-changing Dressings Pickle and Preserve Like a Pro Plant-based Milks Nut Butters Index About the Author Acknowledgements Here It Is... Where It All Began Store Cupboard Essentials Quick and Easy Transformative Toast Toppers Brunch Big Vegan Breakfasts Curry for Breakfast Radical Curries and Delectable Dals World Flavours Comfort Food Incredible Pastas and Risottos Small Plates A Soup for All Seasons Salad Bliss Flatbreads and Pizzas Life-changing Pancake Breads Pure Comfort Something Special Tempting Tarts A Little Lighter Devilish Dips and Sauces Life-changing Dressings Pickle and Preserve Like a Pro Plant-based Milks Nut Butters Index About the Author Acknowledgements Here It Is... Where It All Began Store Cupboard Essentials Quick and Easy Transformative Toast Toppers Brunch Big Vegan Breakfasts Curry for Breakfast Radical Curries and Delectable Dals World Flavours Comfort Food Incredible Pastas and Risottos Small Plates A Soup for All Seasons Salad Bliss Flatbreads and Pizzas Life-changing Pancake Breads Pure Comfort Something Special Tempting Tarts A Little Lighter Devilish Dips and Sauces Life-changing

Dal is my go-to meal in times of need. Although there are many types of lentils that can be used to make dal, I find the easiest and quickest way is to use red split lentils. I like to have a huge jar of red lentils in my store cupboard as I know I can easily make a delicious meal in 15–20 minutes.

I've added coconut milk here for a little creaminess, but feel free to just use water if preferred. The tarka (topping) adds another dimension of flavour and texture. Stir it in at the end, it's an absolute must. I serve my dal with a crisp salad of cabbage and toasted sunflower seeds. Dry-fry the seeds for a minute in a pan, until slightly toasted and nutty – thank you to my friend Malin for this revelation.

Tip: the flavour of the dal improves after a few days, so I'll often make a big batch at the weekend and keep it in the fridge to eat another day during the week. It can also be frozen in containers and will keep for up to three weeks.

Coconut dal *with* cabbage salad *and* toasted seeds

Serves 4

2 tablespoons olive oil
2 teaspoons black
    mustard seeds
1 teaspoon ground turmeric
1 teaspoon ground coriander
1 teaspoon cumin seeds
1 teaspoon dried chilli flakes
1 large onion, roughly chopped
4 garlic cloves, sliced
a thumb-size piece of ginger,
    peeled and finely grated
20 cherry tomatoes or
    4 tomatoes, chopped
350g dried red lentils, rinsed
    and drained
400ml coconut milk
a pinch of ground white pepper
½ teaspoon garam masala
a large handful (about 25g) of
    baby spinach leaves
1 tablespoon coconut yoghurt
    or cream
fresh coriander, roughly
    chopped (optional)
sea salt flakes

Firstly, add the olive oil to a large frying pan and place over a medium heat. Add in the mustard seeds. When they start to pop, add in the turmeric, ground coriander, cumin seeds and chilli. Stir for a few seconds, then add the onion. Fry for 8–10 minutes over a medium-low heat until the onion is soft and browning. Add in the garlic and ginger and stir for another few minutes, then stir in the chopped tomatoes. Cook for a further 3–4 minutes.

Add the lentils and the coconut milk and 500ml of water. Stir well, then turn down the heat to low and put the lid on the pan. Simmer for 30 minutes, stirring occasionally. Add more water to loosen, if needed. Season well with salt and the white pepper. Stir through the garam masala, spinach and the coconut yoghurt.

To make the salad, finely shred both types of cabbage and place in a large bowl. Add the extra virgin olive oil, cider vinegar, sunflower seeds and a pinch of salt. Mix well.

Next, make the tarka. Add the oil to a small frying pan with the red onion. Fry over a low heat for 5 minutes, then add in the garlic. Fry for a further 5–7 minutes, until the onion is soft and caramelised. Add in the

For the tarka topping

3 tablespoons olive oil
1 large red onion, finely sliced
4 garlic cloves, sliced
½ teaspoon dried chilli flakes
1 teaspoon cumin seeds
1 teaspoon mustard seeds
10 curry leaves

For the cabbage salad

¼ medium red cabbage
¼ medium white cabbage
1 tablespoon extra virgin
    olive oil
1 tablespoon apple
    cider vinegar
4 tablespoons sunflower
    seeds, lightly toasted

spices and curry leaves and continue to fry for a further 3 minutes. Turn off the heat and season with a pinch of salt.

Top the dal with tarka and, if using, the coriander, and serve alongside the cabbage salad.

Peanut, sweet potato *and* veg curry

This curry has its roots in Thai cuisine as it's rather like a massaman curry with its deliciously nutty peanut base. My first adventures with Thai food were many years ago when I visited my uncle for a few weeks and we travelled all over Thailand. I managed to get very burnt on that holiday but also tasted massaman for the first time – I was hooked. Here is my version. I've added in lots more veggies for freshness and crunch.

Serves 2–4

400ml coconut milk
3 medium sweet potatoes, peeled
    and chopped into 2cm cubes
100g green beans, trimmed and
    halved diagonally
100g chestnut mushrooms, stalks
    removed and caps halved
60g tenderstem broccoli
sea salt flakes and freshly ground
    black pepper

For the curry paste

100g salted peanuts
2 teaspoons maple syrup
2 tablespoons tamari or soy sauce
zest of 1 lime and juice of 2 limes
a thumb-sized piece of ginger, peeled
    and roughly chopped
1 teaspoon dried chilli flakes
1 lemongrass stalk, tough outer layer
    removed, roughly chopped
1 teaspoon cumin seeds
1 teaspoon ground coriander
1 teaspoon ground turmeric
½ teaspoon ground cinnamon
¼ teaspoon ground cloves
2 shallots, sliced
4 garlic cloves

To serve

toasted peanuts, crushed
fresh coriander, roughly chopped
red chilli, thinly sliced (optional)

Pop all the curry paste ingredients into a food processor
or high-speed blender and blitz to make a paste.

Add the coconut milk, curry paste and 250ml of water to
a large saucepan and stir well. Add the sweet potatoes
and bring to the boil over a medium-high heat. Reduce
the heat to medium–low and simmer for 15–20 minutes.

Next, add in the remaining veg and simmer, covered, for
5–8 minutes or until the veg is cooked but still retaining
some bite.

Ladle into serving bowls and top with lots of crushed
peanuts, fresh coriander, and, if using, the chilli.

Although I've travelled around much of India, I've spent the most time in Kerala. Friendly people, beautiful beaches and of course the amazing food – I'm always drawn back. I'm incredibly inspired by the region's breakfast dishes like dosas and the fresh coconut-based curries.

My homage to Kerala would be a thali, the wonderful platter meal of many dishes. My Rebel version consists of a pretty classic tarka dal, cauliflower curry, green bean thoran and coconut chutney. It's my go-to dinner for when I have friends coming over. Not only does it look impressive but it always goes down a storm. The green bean thoran and coconut chutney can be made in advance and served at room temperature.

Tip: in Kerala, fresh coconut is shredded and used for coconut-based dishes, however I find that desiccated coconut works really well.

Tantalising thali – cauliflower curry, coconut chutney *and* tarka dal

Serves 4

roti (page 63), to serve
freshly cooked rice, to serve
sea salt flakes

For the coconut chutney

50g desiccated coconut
1 teaspoon grated ginger
½ green chilli, deseeded
juice of ½ lime
1 teaspoon rapeseed oil
½ teaspoon black
    mustard seeds
½ teaspoon cumin seeds
4 curry leaves

For the green bean
    thoran

1 tablespoon coconut oil
1 teaspoon mustard seeds
1 teaspoon cumin seeds
8 curry leaves
a pinch of dried chilli flakes

Make the coconut chutney. Place the desiccated coconut in a small bowl and cover with boiling water. Leave to rehydrate and soften for about 15 minutes.

Put the softened coconut (reserving the soaking water), ginger and chilli in a spice grinder or mini food processor. Blitz for 1 minute to form a rough paste, adding a touch of soaking water from the coconut to loosen up the mix if needed. Season with ¼ teaspoon of salt and the lime juice.

Next, heat the rapeseed oil in a small frying pan over a medium heat. When the oil is hot, add the mustard seeds and fry gently until the seeds start to pop. Stir in the cumin seeds and curry leaves, and sauté them in the oil for a few seconds. Add these tempered spices (including their oil) into the chutney and mix well. Set aside.

For the thoran, heat the coconut oil in a frying pan over a high heat. Add in the mustard and cumin seeds, and fry for a few seconds until beginning to pop. Add in the curry leaves and chilli, then stir-fry for 1 minute. Now mix in the beans and turmeric, and season with salt. Cover the pan with the lid and cook for 3–4 minutes, until the beans are tender to bite. Stir in the desiccated coconut and take off the heat. Cover to keep warm and set aside.

200g green beans, topped and
tailed and chopped in half
¾ teaspoon ground turmeric
4 tablespoons desiccated
coconut

For the tarka dal
200g red split lentils, rinsed
and drained
1 teaspoon ground turmeric
2 tomatoes, roughly chopped
25g fresh coriander, chopped
½ teaspoon cayenne pepper
3 tablespoons olive oil
1 teaspoon black mustard seeds
1 teaspoon cumin seeds
10 curry leaves
1 red onion, sliced
1 teaspoon grated ginger
2 large garlic cloves, sliced

For the cauliflower
curry
2 garlic cloves, peeled
1 tablespoon grated ginger
2 tablespoons olive oil
1 teaspoon mustard seeds
1 teaspoon cumin seeds
1 onion, finely chopped
½ teaspoon dried chilli flakes
5 tomatoes, chopped
1 teaspoon ground turmeric
1 teaspoon garam masala
1 small cauliflower (about
200g), broken into
small florets

To make the dal, add the lentils to a large pan and pour in 700ml of water.
Bring to the boil over a high heat, skimming off the froth on the surface of
the water. Stir in the turmeric, reduce the heat to low and simmer for
20 minutes.

Next, add the chopped tomatoes, coriander, cayenne and 1½ teaspoons of
salt. Simmer for another 10 minutes, then stir and turn off the heat.

Heat the olive oil in a small frying pan over a high heat and add the mustard
and cumin seeds. Cook until they begin to pop, then add the curry leaves and
onion. Reduce the heat to medium–low and cook for 10–15 minutes until the
onion is soft and browning. Add the ginger and garlic and fry for 1 minute.
Add half this mixture to the lentils and stir in (keep the other half of the
mixture for the topping).

Make the curry. Crush the garlic and ginger to a paste using a mortar and
pestle (or blitz in a mini food processor).

Heat the oil in a frying pan over a high heat. Add the mustard and cumin
seeds and allow to cook until they begin to pop. Reduce the heat to low, add
the ginger-garlic paste, and stir-fry for 1–2 minutes. Next, add the onion and
chilli and fry for 10–15 minutes, until golden.

Add the tomatoes, turmeric and garam masala, then continue to fry until
the tomatoes turn mushy and are almost dry. (If the tomatoes are not juicy,
sprinkle with a tablespoon or so of water and fry for 2 minutes.) Throw in the
cauliflower and mix well. Cook, covered, for 15 minutes, stirring occasionally
until the cauliflower is cooked. Season with salt to taste.

Top the green bean thoran with the reserved tarka mixture and serve
with the coconut chutney, curry and dal all in separate bowls with roti and
rice alongside.

The magical little chickpea is not only a brilliant source of plant-based protein, vitamins, minerals and fibre, it's also an incredibly versatile – and cost-effective – ingredient. It's not surprising that pulses and beans make up the bulk of many traditional cuisines.

I eat chickpeas most days – in soups, hummus, gram (chickpea) flour breads, curries and you'll even find that I sneak them into many desserts. But here's a classic – chana masala, an easy and delicious meal that can be made in minutes.

Chana masala *with* coconut chutney

Serves 2

300g cherry tomatoes, sliced
400g can of chickpeas, rinsed
   and drained
2–3 tablespoons coconut yoghurt
½ teaspoon coconut sugar, optional
sea salt flakes

For the spice paste
2 tablespoons rapeseed oil
1 large onion, roughly chopped
2 teaspoons cumin seeds
6 garlic cloves, peeled
a thumb-sized piece of ginger,
   peeled and roughly chopped
2 teaspoons ground coriander
¼ teaspoon dried chilli flakes
40g fresh coriander, including the
   stalks, roughly chopped
1 teaspoon ground turmeric

For the coconut chutney
50g unsweetened desiccated
   coconut
a thumb-sized piece of ginger,
   peeled and finely grated
½ small green chilli, deseeded
juice of ½ lime
2 teaspoons rapeseed or flaxseed oil
½ teaspoon black mustard seeds
½ teaspoon cumin seeds
6 curry leaves

To serve
toasted hazelnuts
fresh coriander leaves

Firstly, make the spice paste by adding all the paste ingredients to a food processor, blender or pestle and mortar. Blitz (or pound) to a chunky paste. Set aside.

Next, make the chutney. Add the desiccated coconut to a small bowl and cover with boiling water. Leave for 10–15 minutes for the coconut to rehydrate and soften. Drain and reserve about 125ml of the soaking water.

Add the softened coconut, ginger and chilli to a food processor or spice grinder. Blitz until smooth, and then add some of the reserved coconut soaking water to loosen if needed. Add in 1½ teaspoons of salt and the lime juice.

Pour the oil into a small frying pan and, once hot, add the mustard seeds. Fry gently until the seeds start to pop, then add the cumin seeds and curry leaves. Sauté for a few seconds. Add the tempered spices and oil to the chutney and mix well.

Heat a large frying pan over a medium heat and add the spice paste. Fry for 5 minutes, add the tomatoes and cook for 3–4 minutes, until beginning to soften. Pour in 200ml of water, turn down the heat to medium–low and simmer for 30 minutes.

Finally, add the chickpeas to the pan, stir to combine, then stir in the yoghurt and, if using, the coconut sugar. Taste and adjust the seasoning.

Serve the chana masala topped with coconut chutney, toasted hazelnuts and coriander.

I created this recipe somewhat by accident – a happy marriage of component parts – but I think it works. Here I've used cauliflower, fennel, aubergine and peppers but this is a forgiving dish so feel free to use whatever you have to hand.

The super simple tomato curry can be whipped up in 15 minutes and served over the creamy turmeric hummus, which adds both texture and protein. Don't forget the flatbreads for dipping into the tomatoey goodness.

Tomato curry, roast veg *and* turmeric hummus

Serves 4

For the roast veg
½ medium cauliflower, cut into
    florets
1 fennel head, sliced
1 small aubergine, sliced into
    2.5cm rounds and halved
2 peppers, red and yellow, sliced
2 tablespoons olive oil
sea salt flakes and freshly ground
    black pepper

For the tomato curry
2 tablespoons olive oil
1 teaspoon black mustard seeds
1 teaspoon cumin seeds
½ teaspoon dried chilli flakes
1 teaspoon ground turmeric
½ teaspoon fennel seeds
2 onions, roughly chopped
4 garlic cloves, sliced
a thumb-sized piece of ginger, grated
400g cherry tomatoes, chopped

For the turmeric hummus
400g can of chickpeas, drained
    (reserve 4 tablespoons of the water)
2 garlic cloves, chopped
juice of 1 lemon
1 tablespoon tahini
1 teaspoon cumin seeds
1 teaspoon ground turmeric
2 tablespoons coconut yoghurt
2 tablespoons olive oil

Preheat the oven to 180°C/160°C Fan/Gas Mark 4.

Add the vegetables to one large baking tray or two small baking trays. Toss with olive oil and season well with salt and pepper. Roast the veg for 35–40 minutes, until cooked. Set aside.

Next, make the tomato curry. Add the oil to a large saucepan and place over a medium-low heat. Add in the spices and cook for a few seconds. When the mustard seeds begin to pop, stir for a few seconds, then add in the onions. Fry for 8–10 minutes, until the onions are soft and browning.

Add in the garlic and ginger and stir for another few minutes, then stir in the chopped tomatoes. Turn up the heat to medium, pour in 50ml of water and cook for a further 5–6 minutes.

Meanwhile, add the chickpeas to a food processor or blender with the reserved acquafaba (chickpea water), garlic, lemon juice, tahini, cumin seeds, turmeric, coconut yoghurt and oil. Blitz until smooth and creamy (approximately 2 minutes), adding a little water to loosen the hummus if needed. Season to taste with salt and pepper and blitz again.

Spread the hummus onto a large platter. Layer on the tomato curry then the roast vegetables. Great served with flatbread and slaw.

This is one for the whole family – creamy, mild and totally moreish. It's pretty good on its own, but even better with flatbreads and slaw for crunch. I also like to add chunks of crispy fried tofu to this curry for a texture contrast.

Creamy mushroom *and* chickpea korma

Serves 4

50g cashews, soaked in water
  for at least 4 hours
2 tablespoons olive oil or
  rapeseed oil
1 onion, roughly chopped
1 teaspoon ground turmeric
1 teaspoon cumin seeds
1 teaspoon ground coriander
½ teaspoon ground cinnamon
½ teaspoon ground cardamom
½ teaspoon fennel seeds
⅛ teaspoon ground cloves
1 teaspoon garam masala
¼ teaspoon dried chilli
  flakes, optional
4 garlic cloves, crushed
250g cherry tomatoes,
  chopped in half
500ml coconut milk
400g mushrooms, roughly
  sliced (I used closed cup
  or woodland)
400g can of chickpeas, rinsed
  and drained
2 handfuls (about 50g)
  of spinach
sea salt flakes and freshly
  ground black pepper

To serve
toasted flaked almonds
fresh coriander, roughly
  chopped

To make the cashew cream, drain the cashews and add them to a mini food processor (or use a hand blender) along with enough fresh water to cover. Blitz to a smooth and creamy consistency. Set aside.

Heat the olive oil in a large frying pan over a medium heat and add in the onion. Fry 8–10 minutes, until the onion is soft and browning.

Add the spices, lower the heat and stir for 1 minute. Next, add in the garlic and stir for a few minutes more. Stir in the tomatoes and cook for 5–6 minutes, until they have softened a little.

Pour in the coconut milk and cashew cream. Add the mushrooms and drained chickpeas and simmer over a low heat, covered, for 15 minutes.

Finally, add the spinach and let it wilt down. Season well with salt and pepper to taste and serve the korma topped with flaked almonds and fresh coriander.

Living in Birmingham means that I'm spoilt for choice when it comes to Indian restaurants and we can't go for more than a week before visiting at least one of our favourites. On the menu at one of these is gobi matar keema, an unctuous and delicious dish of soft minced cauliflower and peas. This is my version, fresh yet still comforting. Served with a quick rava dosa (semolina and rice flour crepe) and tomato chutney.

Gobi matar keema
with
tomato chutney
and
rava dosa

Serves 4

2 tablespoons olive oil
1 teaspoon cumin seeds
1 teaspoon ground coriander
1 teaspoon garam masala
1 teaspoon ground turmeric
2 onions, finely chopped
4 garlic cloves, crushed into
   a paste
250g cherry tomatoes, chopped
450g grated cauliflower
50g bunch of fresh coriander,
   chopped including the stalks
250g frozen peas
a pinch of dried chilli flakes
2 tablespoons coconut cream
   or coconut yoghurt
sea salt flakes and freshly
   ground black pepper

For the rava dosa (makes 8)

75g semolina (rava flour)
60g rice flour
25g plain flour
½ teaspoon sea salt flakes
1 teaspoon cumin seeds
½ teaspoon dried chilli flakes
1 tablespoon olive oil, plus
   extra for frying
1 tablespoon coconut yoghurt
½ red onion, finely chopped
a thumb-sized piece of ginger,
   peeled and grated
10 curry leaves, chopped
a handful of fresh coriander
   leaves, roughly chopped

For the tomato chutney

1 tablespoon olive oil
1 teaspoon black mustard seeds
1 teaspoon cumin seeds
½ teaspoon dried chilli flakes
6 garlic cloves, sliced
200g cherry tomatoes,
   chopped in half
¼ teaspoon tamarind paste
1 teaspoon maple syrup

Make the dosa. Firstly, add the flours, salt, cumin seeds and chilli to a large bowl. Stir to combine. Add the oil, yoghurt, onion, ginger, curry leaves, fresh coriander and 500ml of water. Stir well to combine. Cover and allow to sit for 20–30 minutes. (Note – the batter may separate during this time, in that case just stir to combine.)

Meanwhile make the gobi matar keema. Add the olive oil to a large, good non-stick pan and place over a medium-low heat. Add in the spices and cook for a few seconds, stirring, until the cumin seeds pop. Add in the onions and fry for 8–10 minutes, until soft and browning. Add in the garlic and stir for a few more minutes, then add in the chopped tomatoes. Simmer for 5 minutes. Stir in the cauliflower and fresh coriander.

Cover and cook over a medium-low heat for 15 minutes, then add the peas and chilli and season with salt and pepper. Allow to simmer for a further 5 minutes, then stir in the coconut cream.

To make the chutney, add the oil to a small frying pan and place over a medium heat. Add in the mustard seeds. When they start to pop, add in the cumin seeds and chilli, and fry for 30 seconds.

Add in the garlic and stir for a few minutes, then add in the chopped tomatoes.

Cook for a further 5–6 minutes, until the tomatoes have cooked down. Add the tamarind and maple syrup and season with 1 teaspoon of salt. Take the chutney off the heat and allow to cool a little, chop roughly by hand. Set aside.

To cook the dosa, heat a dash of oil in a really good non-stick flat-bottomed frying pan over a high heat. Pour about ⅓ cup of the batter into the pan, tilting to form a thin layer over the base of the pan. Cook for 2–3 minutes then flip and cook on the other side. Repeat.

To eat, scoop up the curry with the rava dosa and have the tomato chutney on the side.

I love Ethiopian food, a relatively recent discovery for me. We first went to a wonderful restaurant in Birmingham a couple of years ago and I have been enamoured with the cuisine ever since.

We pretty much always have the same thing, *yetsom beyaynetu*, a huge vegetarian sharing platter consisting of injera bread (a fermented flatbread) topped with multiple small portions of vegetable-based curries and a pile of spicy lentils in the middle. More squishy injera bread on the side is used to dip and scoop with. It is ideal sharing food, and a healthy and tasty plant-based feast.

Here's my pared-back and quicker version offering berbere-spiced lentils, creamy yellow pea stew and sautéed greens. I serve it with a 'cheat's' injera bread that uses teff flour, soda water and bicarb, which creates little bubbles mimicking that of fermentation – a neat solution when pushed for time.

Ethiopian platter *with* cheat's injera

Serves 4–6

For the spicy lentils
1 tablespoon olive oil
2 onions, roughly chopped
1 teaspoon berbere spice
1 teaspoon smoked paprika
1 teaspoon cumin seeds
a thumb-sized piece of ginger, peeled and finely grated
3 garlic cloves, sliced
2 tablespoons tomato paste
300g red split lentils, rinsed well and drained
1 litre vegetable stock
½ teaspoon ground white pepper
fresh coriander leaves, to serve
sea salt flakes and freshly ground black pepper

For the yellow split pea stew
250g yellow split peas (chana dal), rinsed and drained

To make the spicy lentils, add the olive oil to a large frying pan and heat over a medium heat. Add in the onions and fry for approximately 5 minutes, or until soft and browning. Add in the spices, ginger and garlic, and stir for a few minutes. Stir in the tomato paste, lentils and vegetable stock, bring to the boil, reduce the heat and simmer (uncovered) for 30 minutes. Taste and season well with salt and white pepper.

To make the split pea stew, bring 1.25 litres of water to the boil in a large pan over a high heat. Add the split peas, lower the heat to medium-low and simmer for 45 minutes until soft. Skim off the froth if needed, and add more water if necessary.

In a separate saucepan, heat the oil and fry the onions over a medium-low heat for 5–10 minutes, until translucent. Now add the garlic and fry for a further minute or so. Add the turmeric and cumin seeds, and stir well. Now add the onions to the split peas and cook for a further 10 minutes over a low heat. Season to taste with salt, pepper and chilli flakes.

Prepare the greens. Heat the oil in a frying pan and add the garlic, ginger and spices. Sauté over a low heat for about 30 seconds. Now add the onion and cook for 5–10 minutes, until soft.

Add the greens and lemon juice, and cook for another 2–3 minutes to wilt the greens. Season with salt and pepper. Keep warm.

2 tablespoons olive oil
1 onion, diced
3 garlic cloves, crushed
1 teaspoon ground turmeric
1 teaspoon cumin seeds
dried chilli flakes

For the sautéed greens

2 tablespoons olive oil
3 garlic cloves, finely chopped
a thumb-sized piece of ginger,
  peeled and finely grated
1 teaspoon smoked paprika
½ teaspoon ground cardamom
1 teaspoon ground coriander
½ teaspoon cayenne pepper
  (or more to taste)
1 large onion, finely chopped
150g spring greens, roughly
  chopped
juice of ½ lemon

For the cheat's injera
  (makes 8)

150g teff flour
50g plain flour
½ teaspoon bicarbonate of soda
500ml soda water
groundnut oil, for frying

Finally, make the injera bread. In a large bowl, mix together the flours and bicarbonate of soda. Now pour in the soda water and stir well to form a thin batter.

Heat a non-stick frying pan over a high heat and add a little oil. Add a ladleful of the batter to the pan, tilting the batter to coat the base of the pan. Cook for 2–3 minutes, until the surface is spongy and filled with small bubbles. The edges of the injera bread will begin to curl when ready. (You don't need to flip it.) Repeat until all the batter has been used. The injera is best eaten straight away.

Garnish the spicy lentils with the coriander leaves and serve with the split pea stew and greens on top of the injera.

My friends and I have a favourite ramen restaurant in Shrewsbury. We love ordering lots of dishes, kimchi and wine and the convivial feel of it all. I usually have a bowl of the kimchi fried rice – it's amazing.

Here, cooked rice is fried together with tangy kimchi and good-for-you greens then topped with marinated crispy tofu. If you're in need of a flavour-packed, nutritious and quick meal, this one's for you. And of course it's a brilliant way of using up leftover rice.

Kimchi fried rice *with* greens *and* crispy tofu

Serves 4

1 tablespoon vegetable oil
a bunch of spring onions,
    sliced diagonally
150g mushrooms, stalks removed
6 garlic cloves, sliced
1 tablespoon grated ginger
75g tenderstem broccoli
150g carrots, thinly sliced
20g asparagus, sliced diagonally
100g green beans, halved
75g sugar snap peas, sliced in half
35g kale, tough stems removed
250g pre-cooked rice of choice
100g kimchi (page 262),
    finely chopped

For the tofu

3 tablespoons tamari or soy sauce
2 tablespoons toasted sesame oil
1 tablespoon mirin
1 teaspoon maple syrup
400g firm tofu, cut into large cubes

For the dressing

2 tablespoons sriracha sauce
1 tablespoon tamari or soy sauce
1 tablespoon mirin
1 tablespoon toasted sesame oil

To serve

dried chilli flakes
toasted peanuts
a handful of coriander leaves

First, prepare the tofu. Combine the tamari, sesame oil, mirin and maple syrup in a large container.

Transfer the tofu cubes to the tub, and carefully turn the tofu pieces in the marinade to coat. Allow to marinate for a few hours ideally, or at least 30 minutes.

To make the dressing, add all the ingredients to a jar, replace the lid and shake to combine. Set aside.

Heat a large frying pan over a medium heat and fry the tofu, with a little of the marinade added to the pan, until all the sides are crispy. Remove to a plate and set aside. Wipe the pan out with paper towel.

Heat the oil in the same frying pan and fry the spring onions over a low heat until softened. Add the mushrooms and fry for a few minutes, then stir in the garlic and ginger. Stir-fry for a further minute.

Now add the broccoli, carrots, asparagus, green beans, sugar snap peas and kale, and stir-fry for 3–4 minutes or until the veg is cooked but still retains crunch. Stir in the cooked rice and the chopped kimchi.

Pour the dressing over the rice and mix well. Turn off the heat.

Top the fried rice with the crispy tofu, chilli flakes, peanuts and freshly chopped coriander.

This dish has everything I want – sweet, sticky and slightly salty miso-roasted aubergine on a bed of creamy coconut rice with crunchy green beans and topped with crushed roasted peanuts and fresh herbs. It's pretty special. Inspired by Thai and Japanese flavours, it's a combination that makes a light yet impressive dinner.

Miso *and* maple-glazed aubergine
with sticky coconut rice

Serves 4

2 medium aubergines
2 tablespoons olive oil

For the sticky coconut rice
1 tablespoon coconut oil
6 spring onions, chopped
a thumb-sized piece of ginger,
    peeled and grated
200g basmati rice, rinsed well
    and drained
400ml light coconut milk
sea salt flakes

For the dressing
1 tablespoon maple syrup
1 teaspoon brown rice miso
1 tablespoon tamari
1 tablespoon mirin
1 tablespoon sriracha sauce
1 tablespoon toasted sesame oil

For the beans
1 teaspoon toasted sesame oil
a handful of green beans,
    chopped diagonally

For the toppings
2 tablespoons roasted peanuts,
    lightly crushed
¼ cucumber, sliced into ribbons
a handful of coriander leaves
a handful of mint leaves
1 tablespoon sesame seeds
1 spring onion, sliced

For the rice, melt the coconut oil in a large pan over a medium heat, and fry the spring onions until softened. Add the ginger and fry for a further minute. Now add the drained rice, coconut milk and 200ml of water. Season with about ¼ teaspoon of salt. Stir to combine. Simmer, uncovered, until the liquid is absorbed, then turn off the heat and pop a lid on the rice for 10 minutes.

Meanwhile preheat the oven to 180°C/160°C Fan/Gas Mark 4.

Stir the ingredients for the dressing together in a small bowl.

Preheat two griddle or frying pans. Slice the aubergines in half and score the flesh with a cross-hatch pattern. Add the oil to the pan and place the aubergines, skin side down, for 10 minutes, then flip and cook on the other side for 5 minutes.

Add the aubergines to a large baking tray, skin side down, and then spread the dressing over the flesh side. Bake for 15 minutes, until the aubergines are sticky and browned.

Heat the sesame oil in a frying pan over a medium heat. Add the green beans and stir-fry for 3 minutes, until tender but still retaining bite. Season to taste with salt.

Spoon the coconut rice into bowls and top with the green beans, aubergines and all the toppings.

A sabih is a loaded sandwich of Middle Eastern origin. Layers of textures and flavours – roasted aubergines, tahini sauce, hummus – pile into a soft flatbread. It's completely addictive. One of the best parts is the zhoug – a Yemeni herb and spice condiment that will blow your taste buds if you haven't tried it already.

Roast aubergine sabih

Serves 4

2 medium aubergines, sliced
    into 1cm rounds
3–4 tablespoons olive oil
½ teaspoon smoked paprika
sumac and ground coriander,
    to serve
sea salt flakes and freshly
    ground black pepper

For the flatbreads
200g good-quality white or
    wholemeal flour, plus extra
    for dusting
1 teaspoon baking powder
100g coconut yoghurt or plant-
    based yoghurt of choice

For the zhoug
1 teaspoon cumin seeds
1 teaspoon caraway seeds
1 green chilli, roughly chopped
10g flat-leaf parsley
30g mint leaves
30g coriander, including the
    stalks
3 garlic cloves
6 tablespoons extra virgin olive
    oil, plus extra for drizzling
juice of ½ lemon

For the hummus
400g can of chickpeas –
    reserve 1 tablespoon

Preheat the oven to 180°C/160°C Fan/Gas Mark 4.

In a bowl, toss the aubergine slices in the olive oil, paprika and ½ teaspoon of salt. Arrange in a single layer on a roasting tray (you may need two). Roast for 20 minutes then flip the slices and return to the oven for 20 minutes. Set aside.

Make the flatbread. In a large bowl, add the flour, baking powder and a pinch of salt. Stir to combine. Now add the yoghurt and 75ml of water. Combine thoroughly to form a dough, then transfer to a floured surface. Knead the dough for a few minutes, until springy. Pop it back in the bowl, cover with a damp tea towel and leave to rest for 15 minutes.

To make the zhoug, toast the cumin and caraway seeds in a dry frying pan over a low heat for a couple of minutes, until fragrant. Grind in a spice grinder or use a mortar and pestle.

Put the chilli, parsley, mint, coriander, garlic, extra virgin olive oil, lemon juice and ground cumin and caraway in a food processor or high-speed blender and blitz to a smooth paste. Top with a little more olive oil. Any unused zhoug will keep for several months in the fridge.

For the hummus, add the chickpeas to your food processor or high-speed blender with the garlic, lemon juice, tahini, cumin and olive oil. Blitz until smooth and creamy, approximately 2 minutes, adding a little of the reserved aquafaba to loosen. Season with salt and pepper to taste and blitz again.

To make the tahini dressing, whisk the ingredients along with 4 tablespoons of water in a small bowl. Season with salt and pepper to taste and set aside.

chickpeas for serving and
2 tablespoons aquafaba
(the liquid from the can)
2 garlic cloves, peeled
juice of 1 lemon
2 tablespoons tahini
1 teaspoon cumin seeds
3 tablespoons extra-virgin
olive oil

For the tahini dressing
2 tablespoons tahini
juice of ½ lemon
1 small garlic clove, crushed
to a paste

For the cucumber and
tomato salad
½ cucumber, diced
6 cherry tomatoes, sliced in half
2 spring onions, sliced
a handful of coriander, chopped
2 tablespoons extra-virgin
olive oil
juice of ½ lemon

To assemble the salad, mix all the ingredients together. Season with salt and pepper to taste.

Preheat a large griddle pan or frying pan over a medium heat.

Divide the dough into four portions, then roll out the first flatbread on a floured surface. Pop it on the griddle and allow to char a little, then flip to repeat on the other side. Repeat with the remaining dough. Keep the flatbreads warm on a plate covered with a clean tea towel.

Serve the flatbreads spread with hummus. Top with the roast aubergine, cucumber and tomato salad, zhoug and tahini dressing. Sprinkle with sumac, coriander and the reserved chickpeas.

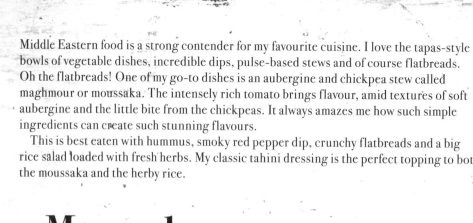

Middle Eastern food is a strong contender for my favourite cuisine. I love the tapas-style bowls of vegetable dishes, incredible dips, pulse-based stews and of course flatbreads. Oh the flatbreads! One of my go-to dishes is an aubergine and chickpea stew called maghmour or moussaka. The intensely rich tomato brings flavour, amid textures of soft aubergine and the little bite from the chickpeas. It always amazes me how such simple ingredients can create such stunning flavours.

This is best eaten with hummus, smoky red pepper dip, crunchy flatbreads and a big rice salad loaded with fresh herbs. My classic tahini dressing is the perfect topping to both the moussaka and the herby rice.

Moussaka: aubergine *and* chickpea stew *with* herby rice

Serves 4

2 medium aubergines, cut into
   2cm dice
5 tablespoons olive oil
1 large onion, finely chopped
4 garlic cloves, sliced
5 large tomatoes, skinned and
   deseeded, or use canned
2 tablespoons tomato paste
1 teaspoon smoked paprika
½ teaspoon cayenne pepper
400g cooked chickpeas, rinsed
   and drained
2 tablespoons finely
   chopped mint
sea salt flakes and freshly
   ground black pepper

For the herby rice

250g brown or white rice,
   cooked
2 big handfuls (about 20g)
   of coriander
2 tablespoons finely
   chopped mint
2 tablespoons finely chopped
   basil or parsley
8 cherry tomatoes, chopped
1 red onion, finely chopped
grated zest and juice of 1 lemon
2 tablespoons olive oil
1 tablespoon sea salt flakes
1 teaspoon dried chilli flakes,
   optional

For the tahini dressing

1 tablespoon olive oil
juice of ½ lemon
1 tablespoon tahini
1 garlic clove, crushed to
   a paste
2 tablespoons water

For the garnish

fresh mint
dukkah (page 252)

Preheat the oven to 180°C/160°C Fan/Gas Mark 4.

Add the aubergines to a large roasting tray and toss them in 3 tablespoons of olive oil. Roast for 30 minutes, until browned.

Add the remaining 2 tablespoons of oil to a large frying pan and add in the onion. Fry over a medium-low heat for 10 minutes, until soft and slightly browning. Add in the garlic and cook for a further few minutes.

Next, add the tomatoes, tomato paste, paprika, cayenne, aubergines, chickpeas and 250ml of water. Cook for about 20 minutes, topping up with more water if needed. Finally, season with salt and scatter over the mint.

In a large bowl, mix the cooked rice with the herbs, tomatoes, onion, lemon zest and juice, olive oil and seasonings.

Add all the ingredients for the tahini dressing to a small bowl and whisk until creamy. Season to taste with salt and pepper.

Transfer the moussaka to a large serving bowl, top with the tahini dressing, lots of fresh mint and the dukkah. Serve with hummus, muhammara (Levantine dip) and flatbreads.

How delicious are gyoza dumplings? These crispy on the outside, soft and gooey on the inside little parcels of joy are totally moreish. They may look complicated but don't fret, they're much easier than they look. You just need a little patience, and don't worry about them looking perfect.

Here I've given you two flavour options – kimchi tofu and spicy mushroom. Both are ridiculously delicious and hugely addictive.

Gyozas two ways: kimchi tofu *and* spicy mushroom

Makes 32

For the gyoza dough
240g plain flour, plus extra
    for dusting
1 teaspoon fine sea salt
125ml hot water
1 tablespoon olive oil
2–3 tablespoons rapeseed oil,
    for frying

For the mushroom filling
2 tablespoons toasted
    sesame oil
a bunch of spring onions,
    finely chopped
6 garlic cloves, finely chopped
2 teaspoons grated ginger
400g mushrooms, finely
    chopped
2 tablespoons tamari or
    soy sauce
2 tablespoons gochujang
    (Korean hot pepper paste)
2 teaspoons mirin

For the kimchi filling
1 tablespoon olive oil
1 shallot, finely chopped

Make the dough. Mix the flour and salt in a large mixing bowl. Add the hot water and olive oil and combine to form a dough. Tip the dough onto a clean, floured surface and knead for a few minutes until springy. Pop the dough back into the bowl and cover with a clean cloth. Set aside for 30 minutes.

Meanwhile, make the fillings. For the mushroom, heat the sesame oil in a frying pan and fry the spring onions over a medium heat for a few minutes until softened. Add the garlic and ginger and stir-fry for a further minute. Now add the mushrooms and tamari, and stir-fry until soft. Stir in the gochujang and mirin. Take off the heat and transfer to a bowl to cool.

For the kimchi filling, heat the oil in a frying pan and fry the shallots and carrot over a medium heat for 4–5 minutes. Next, add the garlic and ginger and continue to stir-fry for a further minute. Add the tamari, maple syrup, vinegar and sesame oil, followed by the tofu, and stir to combine. Sprinkle over the toasted seeds and add the kimchi, salt and chilli flakes. Stir to combine.

Transfer to a large bowl and then mash up a little with a fork. Set aside to cool slightly.

Mix the ingredients for the dipping sauce in a small bowl and set aside.

To make the dumplings, divide the dough into four portions. Roll one of the portions into a tube and cut into eight pieces. Roll each one into balls, then use the palm of your hand to flatten them into a thick discs. Using a rolling pin, roll out to form large discs, about 8cm in diameter. Scoop

½ carrot, finely diced

2 garlic cloves, finely chopped

a thumb-sized piece of ginger,
  peeled and grated

½ tablespoon tamari or
  soy sauce

½ teaspoon maple syrup

½ teaspoon rice wine vinegar

1 tablespoon toasted
  sesame oil

100g firm tofu, diced

1 tablespoon sunflower
  seeds, toasted

35g kimchi (page 262),
  finely chopped

a small pinch of sea salt flakes

a pinch of chilli flakes

For the dipping sauce

2 tablespoons tamari or
  soy sauce

1 tablespoon mirin

½ teaspoon grated ginger

1 tablespoon toasted
  sesame oil

2 tablespoons lime juice

a pinch of dried chilli flakes

a pinch of sesame seeds

1–2 teaspoons of one of the fillings (kimchi or mushroom) and pop it into the centre of the disc. Pull up two edges together at one side then pull up alternative sides, creating a concertina effect, then press to seal along the seam to secure. Pop the finished dumplings on a lightly floured surface and cover with a clean tea towel while making the rest so that they don't dry out. Repeat with all of the dough and the fillings.

Heat 1 tablespoon of the rapeseed oil in a large non-stick frying pan on a medium-high heat. Add the dumplings to the pan (you may need to do this in batches depending on the size of your pan) and fry for 2–3 minutes, until the bottoms are golden.

Now pour 60ml of water into the pan and cover with a lid. Reduce to a medium-low heat and cook, covered, for about 5 minutes. After this time, the water will have evaporated – add a little more oil to fry the dumplings on the other sides if desired. Transfer the cooked dumplings to a plate. Repeat.

Serve the dumplings with the dipping sauce on the side for dunking.

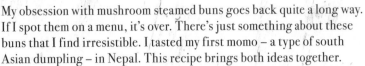

My obsession with mushroom steamed buns goes back quite a long way. If I spot them on a menu, it's over. There's just something about these buns that I find irresistible. I tasted my first momo – a type of south Asian dumpling – in Nepal. This recipe brings both ideas together.

My momos are pretty easy to make. A simple dough packed with a tasty mushroom filling of garlic, ginger, sesame, tamari, miso and hoisin and then steamed to create deliciously soft buns. Perfect!

Hoisin mushroom momos

Makes 8

2 tablespoons toasted sesame oil
½ red onion, finely chopped
2 garlic cloves, finely sliced
½ teaspoon grated ginger
400g mushrooms, finely chopped
1 teaspoon mirin
1 tablespoon tamari or soy sauce
½ teaspoon brown rice miso
2 tablespoons hoisin sauce
a pinch of dried chilli flakes
a twist of black pepper
toasted sesame seeds, to sprinkle
sriracha sauce, to serve

For the dough

100g plain white flour, plus extra for dusting
¼ teaspoon sea salt flakes
1 teaspoon olive oil

To make the dough, combine the flour and salt in a large bowl. Add the olive oil and 75ml of water and mix to form a dough.

Knead the dough on a floured surface, adding more flour as necessary, until smooth. Transfer the dough back into the bowl and cover with a damp tea towel. Let the dough rest for 30 minutes.

Meanwhile, make the filling. Heat the sesame oil in a frying pan and fry the onion for 6–10 minutes, until soft and browning. Add in the garlic and ginger, and cook for a further minute. Stir in the mushrooms, mirin, tamari, miso and hoisin sauce and fry for a further 2–3 minutes, until the mushrooms are cooked. Finally, add the chilli and pepper. Set aside to cool.

Divide the dough into eight portions. Roll each portion on a floured surface into balls (about 20g each) then roll out to create 8cm discs.

Cup a disc in the fingers of one hand and put 2 teaspoons of the filling in the centre. Then pull the dough up around the filling and pinch the edges together at the top so that it's completely sealed.

Place the buns into a bamboo steamer and steam for 12 minutes. The momos should appear transparent when ready. Remove from the steamer and sprinkle with sesame seeds.

Serve with sriracha sauce.

Baked mushrooms *with* cashew cheese *in a* rich tomato *and* pepper sauce

You'll notice that I have lots of mushroom recipes in this book. I love their texture and the fantastic meatiness they add to dishes. The combination of rich tomato sauce, 'meaty' mushrooms and creamy cashew cheese is so tasty here – I think you'll agree.

The recipe looks more complicated than it actually is. It's essentially a really good tomato sauce (that also doubles as a pizza or pasta sauce), cashew cheese (just blending) and some lovely field mushrooms. It's great served with chunks of fresh sourdough or flatbread, good extra virgin olive oil and a crisp green salad.

Serves 4

tomato and pepper sauce
  (page 251)
8 field mushrooms, stalks
  removed
1 tablespoon olive oil
fresh herbs, chopped, to serve
a drizzle of balsamic glaze,
  to serve

For the cashew cheese
150g cashews, soaked in water
  for 4 hours
3 tablespoons nutritional
  yeast flakes
1 tablespoon lemon juice
1 garlic clove, peeled, optional
1 tablespoon apple cider vinegar
½ teaspoon Dijon mustard
sea salt flakes and freshly
  ground black pepper

Drain the cashews and add to a
food processor with the remaining
ingredients for the cheese and
2 tablespoons of water. Blitz until
smooth and creamy.

Preheat the oven to 180°C/160°C
Fan/Gas Mark 4.

Spread the tomato sauce over
the base of a large baking tray
(you could also use two small trays).
Arrange the mushrooms on top,
stalks facing up, pressing down
into the sauce a little. Spoon
1–2 tablespoons of cashew cheese
onto each of the mushrooms,
spreading evenly over the surface.
Drizzle with 1 tablespoon of olive
oil. Roast for 45 minutes, until the
mushrooms are soft. Serve topped
with fresh herbs and a drizzle of
balsamic glaze.

Imagine sitting in the sun at a table laden with fresh and delicious dishes. This aubergine and pesto bake is so full of the flavours of the Mediterranean sunshine it could be the perfect centrepiece. The tomato and pepper sauce is a great companion to the charred aubergines and pesto, making for a lovely summery spread. It's perfect with big salads, bread and dips, and great eaten al fresco.

I know that aubergines are a little polarising so if you're not a fan, this recipe also works really well with thinly sliced roast butternut squash or sweet potato. The choice is yours.

Layered aubergine *and* pesto bake

Serves 4–6

200g chopped hazelnuts
100g rocket leaves
1 tablespoon extra virgin
    olive oil
a squeeze of lemon juice
sea salt flakes and freshly
    ground black pepper

For the aubergines

3 tablespoons extra virgin
    olive oil
juice of ½ lemon
1 teaspoon cumin seeds
1 teaspoon fennel seeds
1 teaspoon dried oregano
2 large aubergines, sliced
    lengthways into 1cm rounds

For the tomato and
    pepper sauce

3 red peppers
2 tablespoons olive oil
1 onion, roughly chopped
4 garlic cloves, sliced
1 teaspoon cumin seeds
½ teaspoon smoked paprika

Firstly put the extra virgin olive oil, lemon juice, cumin and fennel seeds and oregano in a jar with a pinch of salt and shake to combine.

Add just enough of the olive oil mixture to coat the bottom of a large frying pan. Lay the aubergine slices in the pan (in a single layer and in batches if necessary) and drizzle a little more of the oil over the top. Set over a low heat and fry for around 10–15 minutes, then flip the aubergine slices (adding more of the oil if needed) and cook for 10 minutes more. Remove the aubergines and set aside. Repeat with the remaining aubergine slices.

Fry the peppers on a griddle pan over a high heat for 10–15 minutes, turning frequently until nicely charred all over. Set aside to cool, then remove the seeds and chop the flesh roughly (you can save some of the charred skins and add this to the flesh too).

Add the oil and onion to a wide-bottomed frying pan and cook over a low heat for around 10 minutes, or until soft and beginning to brown. Add the garlic and fry for 30 seconds more. Add the cumin seeds, paprika, tomatoes and chopped chargrilled peppers with a pinch of salt. Cover the pan with the lid and cook over a low heat for 25 minutes.

Season with pepper and, if using, add the chilli flakes to the pan and simmer for a further minute.

Preheat the oven to 180°C/160°C Fan/Gas Mark 4.

Put all the ingredients for the pesto into a food processor or high-speed blender and blitz to a chunky paste.

8 large ripe tomatoes or
    30 cherry tomatoes, roughly
    sliced
a pinch of dried chilli flakes,
    optional

For the pesto
about 100g kale, tough
    stalks removed
100g pine nuts, toasted
1 garlic clove, peeled
4 tablespoons olive oil
3 tablespoons nutritional
    yeast flakes

To assemble the dish, spread a little tomato and pepper sauce over the bottom of a large baking tray. Then layer on top half the aubergines, followed by half the pesto and a sprinkle of chopped hazelnuts. Then repeat to create another layer. Finish with a final sprinkle of chopped hazelnuts and a drizzle of olive oil. Cover with foil and bake for 30 minutes.

Toss together the rocket, olive oil and lemon juice and season to taste with salt and pepper, then serve alongside the aubergine bake.

This stew is inspired by both Indian and African flavours. I first made it during winter when all I wanted to eat was warm and comforting bowls of spicy steaming vegetables. It certainly hit the spot, but of course it's fantastic at any time of year.

The stew is this wonderful combination of nourishing vegetables with a creamy nutty sauce, topped with toasted peanuts for crunch. Eat it just as it is or with quinoa or flatbreads.

Sweet potato, cauliflower *and* peanut stew

Serves 4

1 tablespoon olive oil
6 shallots, roughly chopped
4 garlic cloves, sliced
1 teaspoon cumin seeds
1 teaspoon ground turmeric
a small handful (about 15g) of
  coriander, roughly chopped,
  plus extra to serve
6 tomatoes, chopped
400ml light coconut milk
1 sweet potato, peeled and cubed
1 small cauliflower, chopped
  into florets
2–3 tablespoons crunchy peanut
  butter, to taste
juice of ½ lime
1 teaspoon tamari
¼ teaspoon dried chilli flakes
a handful of roasted unsalted
  peanuts, to serve
sea salt and freshly ground
  black pepper

Firstly add the olive oil to a large pan and place over a medium heat. Add the shallots and fry for 8–10 minutes, until beginning to soften and brown. Next, add the garlic, cumin seeds, turmeric and coriander. Stir for 30 seconds or so.

Stir through the tomatoes and cook for a further 5–6 minutes, then pour in the coconut milk and 250ml of water. Add the sweet potato and cauliflower, and stir. Simmer for 20 minutes, covered, until the sweet potato and cauliflower are tender.

Stir in the peanut butter, lime juice, tamari and chilli flakes and season to taste with salt and pepper. Simmer for a further couple of minutes. Top with roasted peanuts and more fresh coriander.

I created this dish when I wanted something super comforting, easy and delicious. It's pretty much made from store cupboard ingredients and vegetables I usually have in the house – tomatoes, peppers, garlic and onions – and it's great after a long day at work as it's a breeze to put together.

Here I've used three types of white beans, tomatoes and a big dollop of coconut yoghurt swirled in to make it beautifully creamy. I love it with chunks of fresh sourdough.

White bean, coconut *and* roast pepper stew

Serves 4

2 red peppers, stalk removed, deseeded and diced
250g cherry tomatoes
3 tablespoons olive oil
2 onions, finely chopped
4 garlic cloves, sliced
5 large ripe tomatoes, chopped
400g can of cannellini beans, rinsed and drained
400g can of butter beans, rinsed and drained
400g can of haricot beans, rinsed and drained
2 tablespoons fresh thyme leaves, plus extra if desired
2 tablespoons coconut yoghurt
a pinch of dried chilli flakes
sea salt flakes and freshly ground black pepper

Preheat the oven to 180°C/160°C Fan/Gas Mark 4.

Firstly, add the peppers and cherry tomatoes to a large baking tray and toss them in 1 tablespoon of the olive oil and a pinch of salt. Bake for 30 minutes or until soft and browning a little. Set aside.

Add the remaining 2 tablespoons of olive oil to a large pan and add in the onions. Fry over a medium-low heat for 8–10 minutes, until soft and slightly browning. Add in the garlic and cook for a further minute.

Next, add the chopped tomatoes, turn the heat down to low, cover the pan with a lid and cook for about 10 minutes, or until softened. Now add in the roast peppers (setting aside the roast tomatoes), the beans, the thyme and 250ml of water. Cover and simmer for 20 minutes.

Season with salt and pepper, and add more fresh thyme if you like. Swirl through the yoghurt and sprinkle with chilli flakes. Top the stew with the reserved roast tomatoes.

Every year, my friends and I rent a big country house and I spend a lot of the time in the kitchen making as many delicious meals as they can physically eat. Over the years I've seen more and more of my friends become vegan and vegetarian, and this substantial and hearty dish where the squash take centre stage is an absolute hit for our Sunday lunches. If this wasn't guaranteed to be on the menu I'm not sure they would actually come!

Here, I've packed the squashes with a nutty mushroom filling, which adds a ton of flavour and a nice contrast to the sweet roast squash. Feel free to add extra veggies, nuts and seeds to make the filling even more substantial and nutritious. Served with roast veg, dips and salad, you'll have yourself a real feast.

Baked squashes *with* a nutty mushroom filling

Serves 4

4 small butternut squashes, halved
2 tablespoons olive oil
2 tablespoons fresh thyme leaves
sea salt flakes and freshly ground
   black pepper

For the mushroom filling
1 large onion, roughly chopped
2 tablespoons olive oil
4 garlic cloves, finely chopped
2 red peppers, deseeded and cut
   into 1cm dice
250g chestnut mushrooms,
   finely chopped
80g kale (about 2 big handfuls),
   tough stalks removed and
   roughly chopped
6 sundried tomatoes, finely chopped
4 tablespoons sunflower
   seeds, toasted
4 tablespoons pine nuts or pumpkin
   seeds if preferred, toasted
1 tablespoon tamari
2 tablespoons nutritional
   yeast flakes
1 tablespoon vegan
   Worcestershire sauce
1 tablespoon maple syrup

Preheat the oven to 180°C/160°C Fan/Gas Mark 4.

Remove the seeds from the squash using a spoon and score the flesh diagonally with a sharp knife. Place the squash on baking trays and rub the flesh all over with the olive oil, then sprinkle with salt and pepper. Place in the oven and bake for 1¼ hours, or until the flesh is tender and the skin golden and caramelised.

While the squash is cooking, prepare the mushroom filling. In a frying pan, gently fry the onion in the oil for around 10 minutes, or until soft and beginning to brown. Add the garlic and fry for a further minute. Next, add the peppers and mushrooms, and cook for 5–6 minutes until the peppers begin to soften and the mushrooms start to brown. Stir in the kale and sundried tomatoes, and cook for 2 minutes. Turn off the heat when the kale has wilted. Set aside.

Blitz the sunflower seeds and most of the pine nuts in a mini food processor, pulsing a few times to form a rough texture. Add the seeds to the pan along with the remaining ingredients for the filling. Stir to combine. Set aside.

When the squash is cooked, load the filling into the cavities, and sprinkle with thyme and the reserved toasted pine nuts.

As soon I as developed this recipe I became somewhat obsessed with it and ate it about four times in two weeks. It's since become a regular feature. There's something so comforting and moreish about the combination of super creamy polenta, rich and earthy green lentils and chunky cauliflower steaks.

Tip: I like to double the amount of lentil ragu and serve leftovers with pasta.

Cauliflower steaks *with* creamy polenta *and* green lentil ragu

Serves 4

1 small cauliflower, sliced into
    2.5cm thick steaks
a drizzle of olive oil
sea salt flakes and freshly ground
    black pepper

For the lentil ragu
2 tablespoons extra virgin olive oil
1 large onion, finely chopped
4 garlic cloves, sliced
100g dark green or puy lentils,
    rinsed thoroughly
1½ teaspoons vegan bouillon
juice of ½ lemon
1 tablespoon balsamic glaze

For the polenta
100g instant polenta
2 tablespoons coconut yoghurt
    or coconut cream
1 tablespoon extra virgin olive oil
1½ teaspoons sea salt flakes
100ml plant-based milk of choice
a pinch of ground white pepper
1 thyme sprig, leaves picked
2 tablespoons nutritional
    yeast flakes
2 teaspoons vegan
    Worcestershire sauce

Toppings
a drizzle of balsamic glaze
dried chilli flakes

Preheat the oven to 180°C/160°C Fan/Gas Mark 4.

Arrange the cauliflower steaks in a single layer in a large roasting tray. Toss with olive oil and sea salt. Roast in the oven for 20 minutes, then give them a turn. Continue to roast for a further 20 minutes, or until the cauliflower is cooked and golden brown. Remove from the oven.

Meanwhile, prepare the lentil ragu. In a saucepan, heat the oil and fry the onion over a medium-low heat for 10 minutes until soft and beginning to brown. Add in the garlic and fry for a further minute. Add the lentils, the bouillon and 500ml of water. Stir well to combine. Turn up the heat and bring to the boil, then continue to boil for 10 minutes.

Turn the heat to low, cover the pan with a lid and simmer for 15 minutes. Finally, add in the lemon juice and balsamic glaze, drizzle with olive oil and season well. Stir to combine.

Next, make the polenta. If using instant polenta, heat 400ml of water in a saucepan and bring to the boil. Slowly add the polenta in a steady stream. Stir continuously for 1 minute. Turn off the heat. Allow to cool a little.

Add the polenta, yoghurt, oil, salt, milk, pepper, thyme, yeast and Worcestershire sauce to a food processor or blender and blitz into a smooth and creamy consistency.

To serve, pour the creamy polenta into bowls or onto plates. Then spoon on the lentils and top with the cauliflower steaks. Add a drizzle of balsamic glaze, and a pinch each of sea salt flakes and chilli flakes.

We've been spending Christmas in Spain for the last few years. I love the crisp mountain air, bright days and freezing nights. Every Christmas Day we head to our friend's house and I usually make a big one-tray bake – like this one – packed with veg and lentils. A perfectly hearty, healthy winter meal.

I finally posted the recipe on my blog before Christmas and it's become one of my most popular recipes – probably because it's incredibly delicious and a brilliant winter warmer. It's definitely good enough to grace your Christmas table.

Ultimate winter roast lentil *and* veg bake

Serves about 6

— whole would be ok

½ large cauliflower, chopped

1 medium sweet potato, peeled and chopped into 2.5cm chunks

3 carrots, peeled and chopped into 2.5cm chunks

2 medium potatoes, peeled and chopped into 2.5cm chunks

2 tablespoons olive oil

2 tablespoons coconut yoghurt or choice of plant-based yoghurt

2 tablespoons nutritional yeast flakes

1 teaspoon Dijon mustard

5 tablespoons extra virgin olive oil, plus extra to drizzle

2 large onions, chopped roughly

4 garlic cloves, sliced

300g dark green or Puy lentils, rinsed and drained

1.5 litres vegetable stock *1 litre*

250g mushrooms, chopped *200g*

juice of ½ lemon

2 tablespoons balsamic glaze

1 tablespoon vegan Worcestershire sauce

1 teaspoon tamari *(soy sauce)*

a handful of walnuts or choice of nuts, roughly chopped *— yum!*

sea salt flakes and freshly ground black pepper

For the caramelised onions

2 tablespoons olive oil

3 onions, finely sliced

Put the cauliflower, sweet potato, carrots and potatoes in one large tray or two roasting trays. Toss with the olive oil and season well with salt and pepper. Roast for 35–40 minutes, or until tender and cooked.

Remove and allow to cool a little. Tip the roast veg into a large bowl and mash roughly with a fork or masher – it's meant to be a very rough mash – then add the yoghurt, nutritional yeast flakes and mustard. Stir to combine and set aside. *This mash is delicious!*

Make the caramelised onions. Heat the oil in a large frying pan and sauté the onions with a pinch of salt for 15 minutes, over a low heat, until soft and caramelised. Set aside.

Preheat the oven to 180°C/160°C Fan/Gas Mark 4.

Heat 3 tablespoons of the extra virgin olive oil in a large pan over a medium-low heat. Add the onions and fry for 8–10 minutes, until soft and browning. Add in the garlic and stir for another few minutes to cook, then add in the lentils and stock. Turn up the heat to bring to the boil, reduce to medium-low and simmer for 10 minutes. Next, turn the heat down to low, then add the mushrooms and continue to simmer for 30 minutes (add a little more water if needed). Stir in the lemon juice, balsamic glaze, Worcestershire sauce, remaining 2 tablespoons of extra virgin olive oil and tamari. Taste and season with salt and pepper.

Add the lentil mixture to a large casserole dish, spreading it over the base of the dish. Spread over the caramelised onions. Top with the mashed veg, spreading it out evenly to cover. Sprinkle with the walnuts and drizzle over extra virgin olive oil. Bake for 20 minutes until nice and golden.

Remove from the oven and allow the bake to cool a little before eating.

I've always loved the changing seasons and because my food naturally veers toward comfort, autumn is a legitimate excuse for me to indulge in making huge pots of stew, dal, curry and soup.

I first had these delicious smoky lentils with my friends and fellow bloggers Sara (aka Shiso Delicious) and Bettina (aka Bettina's Kitchen) while we were on a little getaway in the Herefordshire countryside. We cooked, styled and had fun sleeping in a yurt. It was a completely impromptu meal made with random ingredients, but the dish turned out to be so good I recreated it at home.

I have found the lentils make a pretty perfect combination with my roast harissa cauliflower and aubergine.

Smoky lentils *and* harissa roast cauliflower *with* aubergine

Serves 4

½ large aubergine, sliced into 2.5cm rounds
1 medium cauliflower, cut into 1cm steaks
1 dried ancho chilli
sea salt flakes and freshly ground black pepper

For the harissa dressing
1½ tablespoons rose harissa or 1 tablespoon harissa
3 tablespoons olive oil
1 teaspoon garlic powder
juice of 1 lemon

For the lentils
1 tablespoon olive oil
1 onion, chopped
4 garlic cloves, sliced
300g cherry tomatoes, sliced
350g dried red lentils, rinsed and drained
2 tablespoons tomato purée
a pinch of ground white pepper
½ teaspoon dried chilli flakes

Preheat the oven to 180°C/160°C Fan/Gas Mark 4.

Add the ingredients for the harissa dressing to a large bowl and mix well. Add the aubergine and cauliflower to the bowl with the dressing. Mix well. Add the vegetables to a large roasting tray. Roast for 20 minutes, then turn the aubergine and cauliflower slices over. Continue to roast for a further 20 minutes, until the vegetables are cooked and golden brown. Remove from the oven.

Chop up the ancho chilli roughly, then add to a small saucepan along with 3 tablespoons of water. Place over a medium heat and simmer for a few minutes. Set aside to cool. Add the chilli paste to a mini chopper/blender or pestle and mortar and blitz or crush to a paste.

For the lentils, heat the olive oil in a wide-bottomed pan and fry the onion over a low heat for around 10 minutes, until soft and browning. Add the garlic and fry for 30 seconds more. Add the tomatoes, lentils, tomato purée, ancho paste and 750ml of water to the pan. Cook over a low heat for 30 minutes, stirring occasionally – add more water if needed. Add the white pepper, chilli flakes, tamari and coconut yoghurt to the pan and season with salt. Simmer for a further 5 minutes.

To make the cabbage salad, finely slice the cabbage and place in a large bowl. Add the extra virgin olive oil and cider vinegar, and season to taste with salt. Mix well.

1 tablespoon tamari
1–2 tablespoons coconut
    yoghurt or coconut cream

For the cabbage salad
½ medium white cabbage
1 tablespoon extra virgin
    olive oil
1 tablespoon apple cider
    vinegar
4 tablespoons sunflower
    seeds

Add the sunflower seeds to a small frying pan and dry toast over a medium heat until lightly coloured and smelling nutty. Add to the bowl with the cabbage and toss well.

Serve the lentils topped with the roast veg and the cabbage salad alongside.

When the weather gets colder, is there anything more comforting than risotto? Butternut squash works particularly well in risotto as it melds into the rice, adding sweetness and earthiness.

You don't need huge amounts of butter and cheese to make a super tasty risotto but you do need time – time to slowly cook the onions and to stir in the stock ladle by ladle until the rice is soft and gooey.

On the off chance you have any left over, use it to make arancini balls. I've always loved these crispy balls of soft rice and assumed they were tricky to make, but not at all. It's as simple as rolling in a crunchy, cheesy crumb, then frying in oil and baking for 10 minutes. Voilà – sticky, cheesy, crispy balls of deliciousness.

I like to serve the arancini with a simple but delicious marinara sauce – rich but fresh tomatoes with a hint of oregano and chilli. The sauce is also amazing on pasta or pizza. Give it a go.

Roast squash risotto *or* arancini balls *with* the best marinara sauce

Serves 4

1 medium butternut squash
  or pumpkin (about 600g)
3 tablespoons olive oil
a big pinch of ground
  white pepper
2 onions, finely chopped
4 garlic cloves, sliced
150g arborio rice
2 tablespoons white wine
3 tablespoons fresh
  thyme leaves
1 litre vegetable stock
finely grated zest and juice
  of 1 lemon
1 teaspoon dried chilli flakes
3 tablespoons nutritional
  yeast flakes
1 tablespoon extra virgin
  olive oil, optional
1 tablespoon coconut
  yoghurt, optional
a handful of crushed hazelnuts,
  to serve

Preheat the oven to 180°C/160°C Fan/Gas Mark 4.

Chop off about quarter of the squash and slice into evenly sized chunks – there is no need to take the skin off. Coat in 1 tablespoon of the olive oil, white pepper and season with salt. Arrange in a roasting tray and roast for about 40 minutes, turning occasionally, until nicely golden. Roughly chop and set aside.

Whilst the squash is roasting, add the onions and the remaining 2 tablespoons of olive oil to a wide-bottomed pan and fry gently over a low heat for 8–10 minutes, until soft and browning.

Peel and deseed the rest of the squash and chop into 1cm cubes. Add to the pan with the garlic and fry for a further 5 minutes. Add the rice, wine and thyme leaves to the pan and stir to combine. Pour in about 250ml of the vegetable stock. Turn up the heat a little to bring to a simmer, and then keep adding more stock once the rice has absorbed the liquid. Repeat until the rice is cooked but still has some bite and the squash is tender, about 20 minutes.

Add in the zest and juice of the lemon and season with salt and pepper. Stir in the chilli flakes and nutritional yeast flakes.

If you prefer a soft gooey rice, add the extra virgin olive oil and cover the pan. Allow to sit with the heat off for a further 5 minutes or so.

sea salt and freshly ground
black pepper

For the marinara sauce (optional)

2 tablespoons extra virgin
olive oil
1 onion, finely chopped
3 cloves of garlic, finely
chopped
10 very ripe fresh tomatoes,
chopped or 2 x 400g cans
of tomatoes
2 tablespoons tomato purée
½ teaspoon dried oregano
a pinch of dried chilli
flakes, optional
½ tablespoon coconut
sugar, optional
fresh basil leaves, chopped

For the arancini (optional – makes about 20 balls)

200g breadcrumbs (I use a few
days old sourdough or panko
also works)
1 tablespoon sesame seeds
3 tablespoons nutritional
yeast flakes
a big pinch of dried chilli flakes
1–2 tablespoons olive oil

Stir in the coconut yoghurt, if using, and serve sprinkled with crushed hazelnuts and the roasted squash. Alternatively, leave the risotto to cool a little and then follow the steps below to make the arancini balls.

To make the sauce, add the extra virgin olive oil and onion to a frying pan and fry over a low heat for around 10 minutes, until soft and browning. Add the garlic and fry for 30 seconds more. Add the tomatoes, tomato purée and oregano to the pan and cook for 25 minutes. Season the sauce with salt and pepper, and, if using, the chilli flakes and sugar. Simmer for a further 5 minutes, then remove from the heat and stir through the chopped basil.

Meanwhile, preheat the oven to 180°C/160°C Fan/Gas Mark 4 and make the arancini balls.

Scoop up and squish a small amount of cooled risotto in your hands and roll into golf ball sized portions – try not to make them too big. Place the balls on a plate ready for frying.

Add the breadcrumbs, sesame seeds, nutritional yeast flakes and chilli flakes to a bowl with a pinch of salt. Thoroughly combine, and roll the balls in the mix to coat.

Heat the olive oil in a large frying pan and, when hot, add the balls. Fry over a medium-low heat for a few minutes on each side, until crispy. You may need to do fry the balls in batches, adding a little more oil if needed. Remove from the pan and place on a large baking tray. Bake for 10 minutes.

Plate the arancini and spoon over the marinara sauce to serve.

Amongst the pages of this book you'll find many cauliflower recipes – Cauliflower Curry (page 77), Cauliflower, Aubergine and Garlic Dip (page 256), Cauliflower Soup (page 166) and more. For such a traditional veg, it holds a special place in my heart. It's so versatile and delicious. I would go so far as to say I'm cauliflower obsessed, and I'm hoping that by the end of the book, you will be too.

This recipe showcases the vegetable to the full. Roast cauliflower is blitzed to make a creamy sauce stirred through pasta with crispy kale, and topped with more roast cauliflower for added texture. Absolutely delicious.

If you have a pine nut allergy or intolerance (like my friend Sharon) you can swap the pine nuts for sunflower or pumpkin seeds. The same goes for any pesto.

Roast cauliflower carbonara
with crispy kale

Serves 4

1 medium cauliflower, leaves reserved, broken into florets
3 tablespoons olive oil
1 teaspoon garlic powder
1 garlic head
1 teaspoon rapeseed oil
125g kale, tough stalks removed
225g spaghetti
zest of 1 lemon, plus juice to taste
4 tablespoons toasted pine nuts, to serve
sea salt flakes and freshly ground black pepper

For the sauce

3 tablespoons pine nuts
juice of ½ lemon
200ml almond milk or plant-based milk of choice
2 tablespoons nutritional yeast flakes
½ teaspoon apple cider vinegar
½ teaspoon sea salt flakes
½ teaspoon ground white pepper
2 tablespoons olive oil

Preheat the oven to 180°C/160°C Fan/Gas Mark 4.

In a bowl, toss the cauliflower florets in 2 tablespoons of the olive oil, the garlic powder and 1 teaspoon of salt, and spread on a non-stick roasting tray. Roast for about 20 minutes, then turn. Continue to roast for another 10 minutes, or until tender and golden brown. Remove and set aside.

Meanwhile, add the cauliflower leaves and garlic bulb to a separate roasting tray. Toss with the remaining tablespoon of oil and roast for 20 minutes. Check on the garlic – the bulb should be soft and oozing a little, and the cauliflower leaves tender and crispy at the edges. Remove and set aside.

Put the roast cauliflower florets (reserving a handful of florets to serve), pine nuts, lemon juice, milk, nutritional yeast flakes and apple cider vinegar into a food processor or high-speed blender. Season with the salt and pepper and then squeeze out the roast garlic flesh into the food processor, and blitz until you get a smooth and creamy sauce. Stir through the olive oil and set aside.

Heat the rapeseed oil in a frying pan and sauté the kale until crispy. Season with salt to taste. Set aside.

Cook the pasta in a pan of boiling water, following the packet instructions. Drain, then toss through the cauliflower sauce and kale. Grate in the lemon zest, and a squeeze of lemon juice to taste.

Serve the carbonara sprinkled with the roasted cauli leaves and reserved florets. Finish with the toasted pine nuts thrown on top.

Although big comforting dishes are my usual go-tos, sometimes I need a little bit of elegance in my life. My stylish open lasagne with juicy mushrooms, creamy cashew ricotta and crispy sautéed kale provides just that. Layers of delicious contrasting textures and the final flourish – a luxurious drizzle of truffle oil and sprinkling of toasted hazelnuts. This one has seen many a dinner party.

Open lasagne *with* sautéed mushrooms, cashew ricotta, kale *and* truffle oil

Serves 4

6 dried egg-free lasagne sheets
sea salt flakes and freshly
   ground black pepper

For the cashew ricotta
150g cashews, soaked in water
   for at least 4 hours
3 tablespoons nutritional
   yeast flakes
1 teaspoon apple cider vinegar
½ teaspoon garlic powder

For the mushrooms
   and kale
1 tablespoon olive oil
125g button mushrooms, sliced
4 field mushrooms, sliced
   lengthways
2 handfuls of kale, tough
   stalks removed and
   roughly chopped

For the topping
2 tablespoons toasted
   hazelnuts or toasted
   pine nuts
a drizzle of truffle oil
1 thyme sprig, leaves picked

Drain the cashews and to a food processor or blender along with the rest of the ingredients for the cashew ricotta and 120ml of water. Blitz to a smooth paste. Season to taste with salt and pepper, then set aside.

Bring water to the boil in a large wide pan. Add the lasagne sheets and simmer for 12 minutes or until soft and just cooked in the middle. Drain and refresh in cold water, then place on paper towels to drain.

Heat the olive oil in a small frying pan, add in the mushrooms and fry for a few minutes until softened. Add the kale and sauté for a minute or so until wilted. Season well. Set aside.

Place the lasagne sheets on top of each other then cut in half across the middle. Take two of the half sheets and spread the cashew ricotta on top of each sheet. Place onto two plates. Build by layering mushrooms and kale, followed by another lasagne sheet with cashew ricotta. Repeat to make three layers.

Top with toasted hazelnuts, a drizzle of truffle oil, fresh thyme and a sprinkle of salt.

Beetroot, oh how I love you! Your beautiful red juice and gorgeous earthy flavour, I'm such a fan. Beetroot hummus, beetroot pancakes, beetroot flapjacks, beetroot curry and, of course, beetroot risotto. There is double the beetroot here in fact: cooked tender beetroot through the rice and delicious roasted beetroot on top. Add toasted hazelnuts and cashew 'parmesan' – happy days.

Beetroot risotto *with* caramelised hazelnuts *and* cashew 'parmesan'

Serves 4

2 raw beetroot, cut into small cubes
2 teaspoons rapeseed oil
a pinch of dried chilli flakes
1 onion, finely chopped
3 tablespoons extra virgin olive oil
3 garlic cloves, thinly sliced
350g arborio rice
125ml red or white wine
about 950ml vegetable stock
4 cooked and peeled beetroot
4 tablespoons nutritional
    yeast flakes
juice of ½ lemon
½–1 teaspoon dried chilli flakes
2 tablespoons fresh thyme leaves
sea salt flakes and freshly ground
    black pepper

For the cashew 'parmesan'
250g cashews
4 tablespoons nutritional
    yeast flakes
1 teaspoon garlic powder
½ teaspoon sea salt flakes

For the caramelised
    hazelnuts
60g blanched hazelnuts
1 teaspoon maple syrup
a pinch of dried chilli flakes

To serve
extra virgin olive oil
fresh thyme leaves

Preheat the oven to 180°C/160°C Fan/Gas Mark 4.

Add the raw cubed beetroot to a roasting tray, toss with the rapeseed oil, and season with a pinch of salt and the chilli flakes. Roast for 45–50 minutes, until tender. Set aside.

To make the cashew 'parmesan', Add all the ingredients to a mini food processor and blitz – not too much as you want some texture. Set aside.

Next, put the hazelnuts in a small dry frying pan and toast over a low heat until lightly coloured. Drizzle in the maple syrup and add a pinch of sea salt and the chilli. Remove from the heat and set aside to cool. When cool, place the nuts in a bag and use a rolling pin to crush lightly.

Add the onion and 2 tablespoons of the extra virgin olive oil to a large frying pan and cook over a low heat for 10 minutes, or until the onion is nicely soft and caramelising. Next, add the garlic and stir for a few minutes, then add in the rice and stir thoroughly to coat the grains in oil. Pour in the wine and turn up the heat a little. Let the wine cook off for a couple of minutes.

Add in a ladleful of stock and allow the rice to almost completely absorb it before adding the next ladleful of stock. Continue to add the stock in this way, stirring almost constantly. After a few rounds of adding the stock, chop the cooked whole beetroot into small cubes and add to the rice.

Continue adding stock, stirring occasionally, and cook for 20–30 more minutes, or until the rice is tender. Stir in the nutritional yeast flakes and half the roast beetroot. Add the lemon juice, chilli and thyme, and season well with salt and pepper.

For soft gooey rice, add the extra tablespoon of extra virgin olive oil and cover the pan with the lid. Allow to sit in the pan with the heat off for a further 5 minutes or so.

Top the risotto with the remaining roast beetroot, the cashew 'parmesan' and the caramelised hazelnuts. Finish with a generous drizzle of extra virgin olive oil and a sprinkle of fresh thyme.

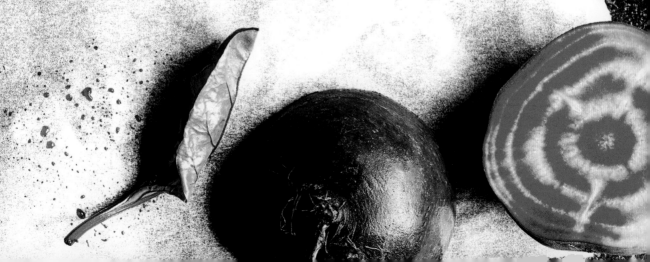

small PLATES, SOUPS and SALADS

Here It Is... Where It All Began Store Cupboard Essentials Quick and Easy Transformative Toast Toppers Brunch Big Vegan Breakfasts Curry for Breakfast Radical Curries and Delectable Dals World Flavours Comfort Food Incredible Pastas and Risottos **Small Plates 143 A Soup for All Seasons 162 Salad Bliss 173** Flatbreads and Pizzas Life-changing Pancake Breads Pure Comfort Something Special Tempting Tarts A Little Lighter Devilish Dips and Sauces Life-changing Dressings Pickle and Preserve Like a Pro Plant-based Milks Nut Butters Index About the Author Acknowledgements Here It Is... Where It All Began Store Cupboard Essentials Quick and Easy Transformative Toast Toppers Brunch Big Vegan Breakfasts Curry for Breakfast Radical Curries and Delectable Dals World Flavours Comfort Food Incredible Pastas and Risottos Small Plates A Soup for All Seasons Salad Bliss Flatbreads and Pizzas Life-changing Pancake Breads Pure Comfort Something Special Tempting Tarts A Little Lighter Devilish Dips and Sauces Life-changing Dressings Pickle and Preserve Like a Pro Plant-based Milks Nut Butters Index About the Author Acknowledgements Here It Is... Where It All Began Store Cupboard Essentials Quick and Easy Transformative Toast Toppers Brunch Big Vegan Breakfasts Curry for Breakfast Radical Curries and Delectable Dals World Flavours Comfort Food Incredible Pastas and Risottos Small Plates A Soup for All Seasons Salad Bliss Flatbreads and Pizzas Life-changing Pancake Breads Pure Comfort Something Special Tempting Tarts A Little Lighter Devilish Dips and Sauces Life-changing

All the lovely Mediterranean flavours here are great served on their own or as part of a mezze. Soft roast veg with creamy and garlicky aioli, crunchy dukkah and tangy yet sweet pomegranate – it's a sensation.

Tip: the aioli is made from aquafaba (the water from a can of chickpeas). This incredible ingredient is an emulsifier, but don't worry too much if the aioli doesn't thicken up. I find that sometimes it does, sometimes it doesn't. But it always tastes delicious.

Roast aubergine *and* courgettes *with* garlic aioli, pomegranate *and* dukkah

Serves 4 as a side

2 small aubergines
2 courgettes
3 tablespoons olive oil
½ teaspoon sea salt flakes
1 teaspoon zaatar
seeds from ½ pomegranate, to serve

For the dukkah

100g hazelnuts
2 tablespoons sesame seeds
1 teaspoon fennel seeds
1 teaspoon caraway seeds
1 teaspoon mustard seeds
a pinch of dried red chilli flakes
1 tablespoon fresh oregano leaves
½ teaspoon sea salt flakes

For the garlic aioli

3 tablespoons aquafaba (the liquid from a can of chickpeas)
1 tablespoon apple cider vinegar
½ teaspoon Dijon mustard
a pinch of sea salt flakes
2 garlic cloves
125ml vegetable or rapeseed oil
1 teaspoon lemon juice

Preheat the oven to 180°C/160°C Fan/Gas Mark 4.

Slice the aubergines and courgettes lengthways into thin strips and tip into a bowl. Pour over the olive oil and sprinkle with the salt and zaatar. Toss to combine. Add the vegetables to a large roasting tray and roast for about 40 minutes, until soft and golden. Remove the tray but leave the oven on.

To make the dukkah, add the hazelnuts and seeds to a baking tray lined with baking parchment. Bake for 10 minutes then remove and allow to cool.

Put the toasted nut and seed mix, chilli, oregano and salt in a mini food processor or spice grinder and pulse on one-second bursts, until you have a rough texture. (Check the texture after each pulse as you don't want it too fine.)

Next, make the garlic aioli. Add the aquafaba, apple cider vinegar, mustard, salt and garlic to a food processor or high-speed blender and blitz to combine. Keeping the food processor running constantly, very slowly drizzle in the vegetable oil. The mixture will become thick and creamy – when it is, stir in the lemon juice. Transfer to a jar with a lid.

Arrange the roast vegetables on a large serving plate, dollop over the aioli and sprinkle over some pomegranate seeds and the dukkah.

Some seriously incredible potatoes here. Crispy and crunchy oven-roasted spuds forked to create ridges that catch flavours, topped with cashew 'parmesan', rocket pesto and dukkah. Brilliant as is or with my White Bean, Coconut and Red Pepper Stew or Moussaka: Aubergine and Chickpea Stew (pages 116 and 100), or simply served with a big crunchy salad.

Crushed potatoes *with* rocket pesto *and* cashew 'parmesan'

Serves 4

750g new or baby potatoes
2 tablespoons olive oil
½ teaspoon dried chilli flakes
½ teaspoon garlic powder
sea salt flakes and freshly ground
   black pepper

**For the sunflower
  seed dukkah**
100g sunflower seeds
1 tablespoon cumin seeds
1 tablespoon coriander seeds
3 tablespoons sesame seeds
1–2 thyme sprigs
1 teaspoon pink Himalayan salt
½ teaspoon dried chilli flakes

For the cashew 'parmesan'
250g cashews
4 tablespoons nutritional
  yeast flakes
1 teaspoon garlic powder

For the rocket pesto
5 tablespoons toasted pine nuts
30g basil leaves
30g rocket
grated zest and juice of ½ lemon
1 garlic clove
2 tablespoons extra virgin olive oil
3 tablespoons nutritional
  yeast flakes

Preheat the oven to 180°C/160°C Fan/Gas Mark 4.

Firstly prepare the potatoes keeping the small ones whole and cutting the larger ones in half into irregular shapes. Transfer to a large roasting tray and drizzle over the olive oil. Sprinkle with chilli and garlic powder, and season with salt and pepper. Bake for 15 minutes then remove from the oven and flip. Return to the oven to bake for a further 15–20 minutes until crispy on all sides. Remove the tray but leave the oven on. Crush the potatoes roughly with a fork and set aside.

For the dukkah, spread the seeds on a baking tray lined with parchment paper and roast in the oven for 5 minutes. Allow to cool.

Tip the seeds and the thyme leaves, pink salt and chilli flakes into a mini food processor or spice grinder and pulse in one-second bursts.

To make the cashew 'parmesan', add all the ingredients to a food processor or high-speed blender and blitz – not too much as you want some texture.

To make the pesto, put all the ingredients in a food processor or high-speed blender and blitz with 2 tablespoons of water until everything is combined to your preferred texture. You may need to scrape the sides down a few times. Season with salt to taste.

To serve, top the potatoes with generous amounts of pesto and a sprinkling of dukkah for crunch, and be generous with the cashew 'parmesan'.

A lovely spring dish of warm roast potato salad with fresh tzatziki, mint and peas. Such a simple recipe. While I love the contrast of the warm crispy potatoes and the cool tzatziki, the whole thing is also rather delicious served cold.

The tzatziki is the hero of the dish – super fresh and creamy. I use it on pretty much anything: dal, savoury pancakes or mixed with some extra virgin olive oil and dolloped onto sourdough toast. Absolutely wonderful.

Roast new potato salad *with* tzatziki *and* peas

Serves 4

500g baby potatoes
1 tablespoon olive oil
1 teaspoon garlic powder
100g frozen peas, defrosted
a handful of fresh mint
a handful of pea shoots
2 spring onions, chopped
a drizzle of extra virgin olive oil
sea salt flakes and freshly
    ground black pepper

For the tzatziki

½ cucumber
120g coconut yoghurt
2 tablespoons chopped dill
2 tablespoons chopped mint
juice of ¼ lemon
1 garlic clove, finely chopped
1 tablespoon extra virgin
    olive oil

Preheat the oven to 180°C/160°C Fan/Gas Mark 4.

Leave the small baby potatoes whole and cut the larger ones into irregular wedges. Add the potatoes to a roasting tray, then coat them in the olive oil, garlic powder and a pinch of salt, tossing them gently. Roast for 40–50 minutes, until crispy on the outside and soft inside.

Grate the cucumber and pop it into a large colander set over a bowl. Leave to drain for 10 minutes. Squeeze out as much moisture as possible then transfer to a large bowl. Add the remaining ingredients for the tzatziki and mix well. Season with salt to taste.

Add the roast potatoes to a large serving tray. Spoon over the tzatziki, and scatter over the peas, the fresh mint, pea shoots and spring onions. Season well with salt and pepper and drizzle with olive oil.

variation

If you want to serve this cold, just let the potatoes cool completely once they're out of the oven and proceed with the recipe.

I created this recipe when I arrived home from work and the fridge was bare, and I mean totally bare. Thankfully there were two little butternut squashes lurking around, but without the necessary ingredients to make any of my other squash recipes, hasselbacks it had to be. If you love hasselback potatoes then you'll love this. There's something really special about those ridges, and the soft yet crispy textures.

These are delicious on their own but are also great as a side dish for curries, dals or a chilli. Pick and choose your topping or mix and match.

Hasselback squash three ways

Serves 4

2 small butternut squashes, deseeded and sliced in half
2 tablespoons olive oil, plus extra to baste
1 teaspoon garlic powder
sea salt flakes and freshly ground black pepper

For the Indian-spiced topping
2 tablespoons olive oil
1 teaspoon black mustard seeds
1 teaspoon cumin seeds
½ teaspoon ground turmeric
3 garlic cloves, sliced

For the caramelised balsamic walnut and thyme topping
50g walnuts
1 tablespoon balsamic glaze
1 thyme sprig, leaves picked

For the chermoula topping
50g coriander, including stalks
2 garlic cloves
2 tablespoons white vinegar
juice of ½ lemon
1 teaspoon ground paprika
1 teaspoon ground cumin
½ teaspoon dried chilli flakes
3 tablespoons olive oil
a pinch of cayenne pepper

Preheat the oven to 180°C/160°C Fan/Gas Mark 4. Peel the squash halves with a sharp peeler, ensuring any white bits are removed.

Add the squash to a large roasting tray and drizzle with the olive oil. Roast for 20 minutes, then remove from the oven and, using a sharp knife, carefully cut ridges on the skin-side of the squash being careful not to cut right through. Baste the squash with oil and sprinkle with 1 teaspoon each of salt and the garlic powder. Return to the oven to roast for a further 50–60 minutes, or until tender. To crisp up the top, pop the squash halves under a hot grill for a few minutes.

To make the Indian-spiced topping, heat the oil in a small frying pan with the spices and garlic. Fry over a medium heat for few minutes, or until the spices are fragrant and the garlic is toasted. Transfer to a small bowl.

To make the caramelised balsamic walnut topping, dry-toast the walnuts in a frying pan over a low heat until lightly golden brown. Remove and allow to cool. Using a pestle and mortar, crush the walnuts a little and add the balsamic glaze and thyme, and season with salt and pepper. Stir to combine.

For the chermoula topping, simply add the ingredients to a food processor or blender and blitz to combine.

Serve the hasselback squash with your chosen topping/s.

The scent of ripe seasonal tomatoes transports me to childhood, sitting in the sun eating whole bowls of them, popping in one after the other.

This tomato tart is a bit of a showstopper – a walnut base topped with a creamy 'cheesy' tomato filling and then beautiful heirloom multicoloured cherry tomatoes. It's baked and then drizzled with olive oil and topped with lots of fresh herbs.

Heirloom tomato tart
with a walnut base

Makes 1 x 23cm tart

sunflower oil, for greasing
about 200g multicoloured
   heirloom tomatoes, halved
extra virgin olive oil, to drizzle
fresh herbs (basil or thyme)
sea salt flakes

For the tart base

2 tablespoons ground flaxseeds
70g walnuts
75g gluten-free oat flour or oats
   blitzed to a flour
60g buckwheat flour
¾ teaspoon sea salt flakes
½ teaspoon garlic powder
1½ tablespoons olive oil
3 tablespoons almond milk
   or other plant-based milk
   of choice

For the filling

150g cashews, soaked in water
   for at least 2 hours
3 tablespoons nutritional
   yeast flakes
2 tablespoons lemon juice
1 teaspoon garlic powder
1 tablespoon Dijon mustard
4 cherry tomatoes, sliced
400g chickpeas, rinsed
   and drained
1 teaspoon sea salt

Preheat the oven to 180°C/160°C Fan/Gas Mark 4 and grease a 23cm loose-bottomed tin with sunflower oil.

Make the flax 'egg' by mixing the ground flaxseeds and 4 tablespoons of water in a small bowl. Set aside for 5 minutes to thicken.

Add the walnuts to a mini food processor and blitz until you get a fine meal. Tip the ground walnuts, oat and buckwheat flours, salt and garlic powder into a large bowl and mix to combine. Add the olive oil, milk and flax 'egg'. Mix thoroughly to form a dough.

Transfer the dough to the prepared tin and use your fingers to press it into the base and up the sides. Use a fork to poke a few holes across the base. Bake for 10 minutes, then remove from the oven (leaving the oven on) and leave to sit while you make the filling.

Drain the cashews and add to a food processor or high-speed blender along with 60ml of water and the remaining ingredients for the filling. Blitz until smooth and creamy. Layer the mixture across the bottom of the tart. Arrange the tomatoes on top, pressing them into the filling mixture a little. Drizzle with a little extra virgin olive oil and sprinkle with salt flakes.

Return to the oven and bake for 30 minutes until the filling is firm to touch. Remove the tart and allow to cool completely before carefully removing from the tin and onto a plate.

Serve sprinkled with your fresh herbs, and anointed with extra virgin olive oil.

Roast broccoli
with satay dressing

We all agree that roast cauliflower is a winner,
but have you tried roast broccoli? It becomes
beautifully nutty on the outside and soft on the
inside. Paired with satay dressing, which brings
out broccoli's nutty flavour, it's next level. I
would be happy eating roast broc on its own, but
it does work really well as a side for any curry
(pages 70–87), for Kimchi Tofu Gyozas (page
102) and, my particular favourite, with Miso
and Maple-glazed Aubergine (page 95).

Tip: make a double batch of the satay sauce and
use leftovers in stir-fries, doused over crispy tofu
or sautéed greens.

Serves 2–4

2 broccoli heads, cut into 2cm
   thick steaks
2 tablespoons olive oil
toasted salted peanuts
a handful of coriander (about
   15g), roughly chopped
a pinch of dried chilli
   flakes, optional
sea salt flakes

For the satay dressing

1 tablespoon tamari
1 teaspoon sriracha sauce
2 tablespoons toasted
   sesame oil
3 tablespoons coconut milk
1 teaspoon maple syrup
¼ teaspoon brown rice miso
2 tablespoons crunchy
   peanut butter
½ teaspoon garlic granules
½ teaspoon dried chilli flakes

Preheat the oven to 180°C/
160°C Fan/Gas Mark 4.

Divide the broccoli steaks
between two roasting trays
and toss with the olive oil and a
generous pinch of salt. Place in
the oven to cook for 15 minutes,
then flip over and continue
cooking for a further 15 minutes,
or until the broccoli steaks are
crispy on the outside and tender
in the middle.

To make the dressing, put the
ingredients into a large bowl or
lidded jar and mix/shake well
to combine.

When ready to serve, toss
the broccoli with the dressing,
peanuts, coriander and, if using,
the chilli flakes.

I'm a huge lover of wholesome comfort foods like stews, soups and curries, but sometimes I crave a big bowl of crunchy slaw.

This one is packed with multicoloured veg, a sesame-soy dressing and crunchy toasted seeds, topped with juicy pomegranate seeds and creamy avocado. It's bursting with both flavour and nutrition.

Rainbow slaw *with* miso dressing, avocado *and* toasted seeds

Serves 4

¼ red cabbage, finely shredded
1 carrot, sliced into fine
    matchsticks
½ fennel bulb, finely sliced
4 spring onions, sliced
    diagonally
1 avocado, peeled, destoned
    and sliced
4 tablespoons pomegranate
    seeds
a handful of coriander leaves
black sesame seeds, to sprinkle

For the toasted seeds
3 tablespoons sunflower seeds
2 tablespoons pumpkin seeds
1 tablespoon sesame seeds

For the miso dressing
1 tablespoon tamari
½–1 teaspoon brown rice miso
2 tablespoons lime juice
1 tablespoon toasted
    sesame oil
a thumb-sized piece of ginger,
    peeled and finely grated
1 tablespoon maple syrup
a pinch of dried chilli flakes

Dry-toast the seeds in a frying pan over a medium heat, until lightly toasted. Set aside.

To make the dressing, add all the ingredients to a jar along with 3 tablespoons of water. Replace the lid and shake to combine.

Add the cabbage, carrot, fennel and spring onions to a large bowl.

Toss the veg with the dressing, then top with the sliced avocado, pomegranate seeds and the toasted seeds. Sprinkle with fresh coriander and black sesame seeds and serve.

A tray bake is one of the easiest meals but there's no skimping on flavour here. Roast your veg, add some chickpeas for protein and then top with a creamy basil and cashew cream. It's an easy and healthy weekday meal, and any leftovers are perfect for packed lunches. I like baby potatoes or sweet potatoes, but use whatever veg you have to hand.

Ultimate roast veg *and* chickpea tray bake *with* basil-cashew cream

Serves 4–6

½ large squash (500g), peeled, deseeded and chopped into 2cm cubes
1 red pepper, deseeded and sliced into strips
1 aubergine, cubed
1 red onion, sliced
½ fennel bulb, sliced
8 garlic cloves, sliced
extra virgin olive oil
a drizzle of balsamic vinegar
500g cherry tomatoes
2 handfuls (70g) of kale, tough stalks removed
400g can of chickpeas, rinsed and drained
sea salt flakes and freshly ground black pepper

For the basil-cashew cream

175g cashews, soaked in water for at least 4 hours
1 garlic clove, peeled
juice of 1 lemon
1 tablespoon olive oil
25g basil leaves

To serve

a squeeze of lemon juice
1 tablespoon toasted pine nuts
a small handful of basil leaves

Preheat the oven to 180°C/160°C Fan/Gas Mark 4.

Into a large roasting tray, or divided between two, add the squash, pepper, aubergine, onion, fennel and garlic. Toss with a good glug of extra virgin olive oil and balsamic vinegar, and season with salt and pepper. Add a splash of water.

Transfer to the oven and roast for 30 minutes, then remove the tray and toss in the tomatoes, kale and chickpeas. Drizzle with more oil and season with a pinch of sea salt. Roast for another 30–45 minutes or until the vegetables are soft and the tomatoes have burst and are sticky.

To make the basil-cashew cream, drain the cashews and put all the ingredients in a food processor or high-speed blender with 100ml of water. Blitz until smooth and creamy.

Serve with the basil-cashew cream, a drizzle of extra virgin olive oil and a squeeze of lemon, and finally scatter with toasted pine nuts and fresh basil.

Tamarind is both sweet and tart. It's one of my favourite tastes and I thought it would make a delicious base for roast potatoes. I was right. The sticky spiced tamarind makes an incredibly delicious coating for the crispy roast potatoes. Enjoy!

Sticky tamarind potatoes

Serves 4

750g salad potatoes
2 tablespoons olive oil
1 onion, roughly chopped
3 garlic cloves, sliced
a thumb-sized piece of ginger,
     peeled and chopped
1 green chilli, chopped
1 teaspoon cumin seeds
½ teaspoon fennel seeds
1 teaspoon ground coriander
4 tomatoes, roughly chopped
2 teaspoons coconut sugar or
     maple syrup
1 teaspoon tamarind
     concentrate
a large handful of fresh
     coriander, chopped, to serve
sea salt flakes and freshly
     ground black pepper

Preheat the oven to 180°C/160°C Fan/Gas Mark 4.

Firstly prepare the potatoes, keeping small ones whole and cutting larger ones in half or into irregular shapes. Transfer to a large roasting tray and drizzle 1 tablespoon of the olive oil over the top. Sprinkle with salt and pepper. Roast for 15 minutes then remove from the oven and flip. Return to the oven to roast for a further 15–20 minutes, until crispy on all sides.

In a mini food processor, blitz the onion, garlic, ginger and chilli to a purée.

Heat the remaining tablespoon of oil in a frying pan over a medium-low heat. Cook the cumin and fennel seeds for a minute until they pop. Add the ground coriander and cook for a minute, then add the onion-garlic purée. Reduce the heat to low and cook, stirring, for 5 minutes. Add the tomatoes, sugar and tamarind, and simmer for 20 minutes.

Add the potatoes and a splash of water, cover with a lid and cook until the potatoes are completely tender but still holding their shape. Top with the coriander to serve.

Spring – super green pea *and* mint soup

This super green pea and mint soup is my go-to when I need something nourishing and delicious. It was one of the first recipes on my blog, and I wanted to include it in the book as it's incredibly simple to make, healthy and fresh-tasting. I like to pack in as many greens as possible (spinach, courgette – you name it) to add to the soup's virtuousness.

Serves 4

1 tablespoon olive oil
2 onions, roughly chopped
1 courgette, chopped
200g sugar snap peas, chopped
150g greens beans
3 garlic cloves, sliced
1 tablespoon vegetable
    stock powder such as
    vegan Swiss bouillon
500g frozen peas
70g spinach
a handful (15g) of mint leaves
sea salt and freshly ground
    black pepper

To serve
50g peas, optional
herby tahini dressing
    (page 259)
15g pine nuts

Heat the olive oil in a saucepan and
fry the onions for 7–8 minutes over
a medium-low heat until soft.

Add the courgette, sugar snap
peas and green beans, and fry for
2 minutes. Next, add the garlic
and cook for a further minute. Mix
the stock powder with 1 litre of
just-boiled water and pour into the
pan. Turn up the heat and bring to
the boil. Reduce the heat and then
throw in the frozen peas and the
spinach – when the spinach has
wilted, take the pan off the heat and
add the mint, and season with salt
and pepper.

Using a hand blender or food
processor, blitz until smooth.

This soup is delicious topped with
peas, tahini dressing and pine nuts,
and some sourdough or flatbread.

One of my earliest food memories is eating cherry tomatoes (and peas) – given to my sister and me by one of our neighbours. Every year he seemed to have an abundance and he shared his spoils. My tomato soup is rich and intensely tomatoey. Roasting the tomatoes first with garlic and red peppers intensifies the flavour so you end up with an incredible tasting soup. Topped with chunky sourdough croutons, fresh dill and basil pesto and some avocado, this can't fail to taste like sunshine.

Tip: prior to adding water, the soup is actually an incredibly delicious pasta sauce too!

Summer – roast tomato soup
with dill pesto croutons *and* avocado

Serves 4

2 large red peppers
900g ripe cherry tomatoes
1 head of garlic
2 tablespoons olive oil
35g basil
1 tablespoon extra virgin
   olive oil
1 teaspoon balsamic vinegar
1 teaspoon dried chilli flakes
2 tablespoons coconut yoghurt
   or coconut cream, optional
1 chunky slice sourdough or
   wholemeal bread
sea salt flakes and freshly
   ground black pepper

For the dill pesto
20g dill
15g basil leaves
juice of ½ lemon
4 tablespoons olive oil
2 tablespoons toasted pine nuts
2 tablespoons nutritional
   yeast flakes

For the toppings
dried chilli flakes
1 avocado, destoned and cubed
a drizzle of extra virgin olive oil
4 tablespoons toasted sesame
   seeds, or seeds of choice

Preheat the oven to 180°C/160°C Fan/Gas Mark 4.

Remove the stalks and seeds from the peppers and chop roughly. Arrange on a roasting tray with the cherry tomatoes and the garlic, then drizzle with olive oil and season with salt. Place in the oven and roast for 40 minutes. Remove from the oven and leave to cool. Once cool enough to handle, peel the garlic and mash in a bowl.

Add the roast tomatoes, peppers (and their juices), garlic and basil to a large saucepan. Pour in 125ml of water and set the pan over a low heat. Allow to come up to a simmer and cook for 20 minutes. Stir in the extra virgin olive oil, balsamic vinegar and chilli, and season with salt and pepper. Blitz using a hand blender bearing in mind you still want the soup to be a bit chunky. Add the yoghurt and stir in.

Make the pesto by adding the ingredients to a mini food processor, and blitz to a chunky paste. Season to taste with salt and pepper.

Toast the sourdough and cut into chunky croutons.

Serve the soup in bowls topped with croutons, chilli, avocado, pesto, a drizzle of extra virgin olive oil and toasted sesame seeds.

Autumn – creamy roast cauliflower, butter bean *and* thyme soup

The two components – cauliflower and butter beans – make this soup super creamy. I love using seasonal organic ingredients where possible and I originally made this recipe for Organic UK, also known as the Organic Trade Board – a cause I'm really passionate about.

I've tweaked the original recipe by adding butter beans and caramelised hazelnuts but the principle is the same – a deliciously wholesome soup celebrating seasonal organic vegetables.

Organic UK

I've been working with Organic UK for a few years now. They are a membership organisation first set up in 2009 with the aim of increasing organic sales by working with members, press and government bodies.

I've had the pleasure of working on their *Organic. Feed Your Happy* campaign for a while. It's all about making organic an everyday choice, and sustaining that choice in the long term too. Nothing makes me happier than sharing my passion for seasonal, quality, organic food, and it's something I'm proud to be involved with.

Serves 8

2 small cauliflowers, broken
   into florets
2 tablespoons olive oil, plus
   extra to drizzle
4 garlic cloves, unpeeled
1 tablespoon extra-virgin olive
   oil, plus extra to drizzle
1 red onion, finely chopped
4 teaspoons thyme leaves, plus
   extra to serve
1 litre vegetable stock
300ml almond milk or plant-
   based milk of choice
3 tablespoons coconut yoghurt
200g canned butter beans, rinsed
   and drained
3 tablespoons nutritional yeast
   flakes, optional
1 teaspoon apple cider vinegar
a pinch of dried chilli flakes
sea salt flakes and freshly ground
   black pepper

For the crispy butter beans

200g canned butter beans, rinsed
   and drained
2 teaspoons olive oil

**For the caramelised
  hazelnuts**

3 tablespoons hazelnuts
1 teaspoon maple syrup

Preheat the oven to 180°C/160°C Fan/Gas Mark 4.

Add the cauliflower to a large roasting tray (you may need two). Drizzle with 1 tablespoon of the olive oil and season well with salt and pepper. Add the garlic cloves to the tray and bake for approximately 20 minutes. Remove the garlic cloves (don't discard them) and toss the cauliflower. Bake for another 20 minutes, or until crispy on the outside and soft inside.

For the crispy butter beans, tip the beans into a separate roasting tray and drizzle with the oil. Season well with salt and pepper. Roast in the oven for 15 minutes, until crisp and browned, then set aside.

Meanwhile, heat the extra virgin olive oil in a large pan and fry the onion over a medium heat for 8–10 minutes, until soft and browning. Add the cauliflower, minus a small handful for the topping. Squeeze the roasted garlic flesh from the skins and add to the pan along with the rest of the ingredients. Simmer for a few minutes, then blitz using a hand blender until smooth. Alternatively, transfer to a food processor or high-speed blender and blitz. Return the soup to the pan to heat through.

Dry toast the hazelnuts in a small frying pan, then add in the maple syrup and a pinch of salt. Roughly chop and set aside.

Serve the soup topped with the crispy butter beans, reserved roasted cauliflower, caramelised hazelnuts, extra thyme leaves and a drizzle of extra virgin olive oil.

My chickpea soup is packed full of gorgeous spices, tomatoes and nourishing lentils, all the flavours of my favourite dal.

I remember the first time I tasted dal. I was in sixth form and we all decided to take a trip to the local curry house. It was also my first balti experience. Not long after that I went to India and my mind was blown with all the incredible vegetarian delights.

I like to make a big batch and portion it up for quick lunches, served with flatbreads for scooping.

Winter – lemony spiced lentil *and* chickpea soup *with* coriander dressing

Serves 8

2 tablespoons olive oil
2 onions, chopped
3 garlic cloves, sliced
a thumb-sized piece of ginger, peeled and grated
1 teaspoon black mustard seeds
1 teaspoon cumin seeds
1 teaspoon ground turmeric
1 teaspoon ground coriander
½ teaspoon dried chilli flakes
4–5 curry leaves
250g red split lentils, rinsed and drained
400g can of chopped tomatoes
400g can of chickpeas, rinsed and drained
100g spinach, or kale with tough stalks removed
juice of ½ lemon
2–3 tablespoons coconut yoghurt or coconut cream, optional
fresh coriander leaves
sea salt flakes and freshly ground black pepper

For the coriander dressing
juice of ½ lemon
25g coriander
1 tablespoon tahini
1 tablespoon extra virgin olive oil

Heat the olive oil in a large pan and sauté the onions, over a low heat, for 10 minutes, until softening. Add in the garlic, ginger, spices and curry leaves. Fry for a further few minutes. Add the lentils along with 1.25 litres of water. Stir in the tomatoes and bring to a boil over a medium-high heat. Reduce the heat to medium-low and simmer the soup for 20 minutes.

Finally, add in the chickpeas and spinach and squeeze in the lemon juice. If using, dollop in the coconut yoghurt. Season with salt and pepper.

Make the dressing by adding the ingredients along with 50ml of water to a mini food processor and blitzing until creamy.

Serve the soup with generous amounts of dressing and some fresh coriander to garnish.

When I eat this, I imagine I'm on the terrace at our friend's house in Spain. The sun is shining and the table is full to the brim with food … and I'm having a nice glass of wine of course! It always amazes me how food can be so evocative.

This salad is a bit of a showstopper – fresh and beautifully colourful tomatoes, on a bed of creamy aioli topped with crunchy sunflower seed crumble – and it's perfect with bruschetta or tomato bread.

Multicoloured tomato salad
with sunflower seed crumble
and aioli

Serves 2

2 plum tomatoes
10 multicoloured cherry
    tomatoes, preferably
    heirloom, sliced randomly
fresh thyme leaves, to serve
sea salt flakes and freshly
    ground black pepper

For the sunflower
seed crumble

75g sunflower seeds
2 tablespoons nutritional
    yeast flakes
¼ teaspoon garlic powder
½ teaspoon caraway seeds
2 tablespoons extra virgin
    olive oil

For the garlic aioli

3 tablespoons aquafaba
    (liquid drained from a can
    of chickpeas)
1 tablespoon cider vinegar
½ teaspoon Dijon mustard
2 garlic cloves
125ml vegetable or
    rapeseed oil
1 teaspoon lemon juice

Firstly, make the sunflower seed crumble. Dry toast the sunflower seeds in a small frying pan, being careful not to burn them. Remove and set aside to cool a little.

Add the sunflower seeds, nutritional yeast flakes, ½ teaspoon of salt, garlic powder, caraway seeds and pepper to a mini food processor and pulse a few times until you get a rough crumb. Tip into a bowl and stir in the extra virgin olive oil.

To make the aioli, add the aquafaba, vinegar, mustard and garlic to a mini food processor. Blitz to combine. Keeping the machine running constantly, very slowly drizzle in the vegetable oil. The mixture will become think and creamy. At this point, stir in the lemon juice and season to taste. Transfer to a jar with a lid.

Add the tomatoes to a serving bowl, arranging them at random. Sprinkle over the sunflower seed crumb and then drizzle with the garlic aioli. Top with fresh thyme.

Gado gado, the delicious Indonesian salad served with peanut sauce and fried tofu, is my kind of healthy food. I've opted for a stir-fry version, packed with vegetables and the most incredible peanut sauce. Top with super crispy tofu for an amazing flavour and texture combination.

Gado Gado
with
crispy tofu

Serves 4

400g firm tofu, cut into large cubes
2 tablespoons olive oil
a bunch of spring onions, chopped
    into 5cm lengths on the diagonal
2 carrots, cut into matchsticks
3 garlic cloves, sliced
a thumb-sized piece of ginger,
    peeled and grated
100g green beans, trimmed and
    sliced in half
100g tenderstem broccoli
150g button mushrooms, stalks
    removed and sliced in half
¼ cauliflower head, broken into
    small florets
1 tablespoon rapeseed oil

For the dressing
3 tablespoons tamari or soy sauce
2 tablespoons toasted sesame oil
1 tablespoon mirin
1 teaspoon maple syrup
1 tablespoon lime juice

For the peanut sauce
4 tablespoons crunchy
    peanut butter
3 teaspoons tamari
1 tablespoon maple syrup
juice of ½ lime
1 teaspoon tamarind paste
1 tablespoon sriracha sauce
½ teaspoon garlic powder
1 tablespoon grated ginger

Combine all the ingredients for the dressing in a large bowl. Transfer the tofu to the bowl and stir. Allow to marinate for, ideally, a few hours or at least 30 minutes.

Make the peanut sauce. Add all the ingredients to a jar. Replace the lid and shake to combine.

Now add the olive oil to a large frying pan or wok and place over a medium heat. Add in the spring onions and carrots and stir-fry for approximately 5 minutes. Now add the garlic and ginger. Continue to stir-fry for a few minutes. Add 2 tablespoons of the peanut sauce, followed by the green beans, broccoli, mushrooms and cauliflower, and stir-fry for around 5 more minutes. Set aside.

While the veg is cooking, heat the rapeseed oil in another frying pan. Fry the marinated tofu for a few minutes on each side until brown and crispy, then transfer to a plate.

To serve, divide the veg and tofu among four bowls. Drizzle over the remaining peanut sauce and sprinkle with roasted peanuts, fresh coriander and chilli flakes.

3 tablespoons coconut milk or
    2 tablespoons coconut cream
    or coconut yoghurt
2 teaspoons toasted sesame oil

To serve
3 tablespoons roasted peanuts
a handful of fresh coriander,
    chopped
a pinch of dried chilli flakes

I know some of us struggle to eat salad during the winter months but if you add enough nourishing and substantial ingredients like here, in my roast carrot and puy lentil salad, you can absolutely eat salad throughout the year and this one is great hot or cold.

Earthy, comforting lentils combined with soft, sticky roast carrots, peppery rocket and balsamic walnuts – this is feel-good food packed with flavour.

I like to make double the amount of balsamic walnuts as they make an absolutely moreish snack.

Warm, roast carrot salad *with* herby lentils *and* balsamic walnuts

Serves 4–6

8 heritage carrots, chopped in
   half if very large (I like to use
   multicoloured carrots)
1 tablespoon olive oil
rocket leaves, to serve
sea salt flakes and freshly
   ground black pepper

For the lentils
1 tablespoon olive oil
1 large onion, finely chopped
3 garlic cloves, sliced
1 teaspoon chipotle paste
   or ½ teaspoon dried
   chipotle flakes
250g cherry tomatoes, chopped
150g dark green French or puy
   lentils, rinsed and drained
1 tablespoon balsamic glaze
1 tablespoon extra virgin
   olive oil
2 tablespoons fresh
   thyme leaves

For the balsamic
   walnuts
50g walnuts
1 tablespoon balsamic glaze

Preheat the oven to 180°C/160°C Fan/Gas Mark 4.

Place the carrots on a roasting tray and toss with olive oil, then season with salt and pepper. Roast for 50–60 minutes until soft in the middle and caramelised.

Heat the oil in a wide-bottomed frying pan and fry the onion over a low heat for around 10 minutes, until soft and browning. Add the garlic and fry for 30 seconds more, then add the chipotle paste. Next add the tomatoes, lentils, balsamic glaze and 750ml of water, and stir to combine. Turn up the heat and bring to the boil, then reduce the heat and simmer for 40 minutes. Season with salt and pepper and continue to cook for a further minute. Turn off the heat and stir in the extra virgin olive oil and thyme.

Dry toast the walnuts in a small frying pan, then add in the balsamic glaze, and season with salt and pepper. Set aside.

To serve, spoon the lentils into bowls, and top with the roasted carrots, lots of rocket and the balsamic walnuts. Eat warm or at room temperature.

I've cooked this recipe many times at workshops and events as it's easy to whip up and is a real crowd pleaser. All you need to do is roast the veg – cauliflower, fennel, carrots and squash – then dress the butter beans in a lemony zaatar dressing. Mix everything together, drizzle with tahini dressing and top with crunchy dukkah. Perfection.

Roast veg salad *with* butter beans *and* hazelnut dukkah

Serves 4–6

1 small cauliflower, chopped
2 fennel heads, sliced into thin strips
6 carrots, sliced
1 small or ½ medium butternut squash, seeds removed and cut into 2.5cm cubes
2 garlic heads, sliced in half horizontally
2 tablespoons olive or rapeseed oil
400g can of butter beans, rinsed and drained
a big handful each of fresh coriander, mint, dill and thyme, to serve
sea salt flakes and freshly ground black pepper

For the dukkah
40g blanched hazelnuts
1 teaspoon caraway seeds
1 teaspoon fennel seeds
1 teaspoon mustard seeds
1 teaspoon cumin seeds
a pinch of dried chilli flakes

For the zaatar dressing
juice of ½ lemon
1 tablespoon zaatar
2 garlic cloves, crushed
2 tablespoons extra virgin olive oil
1 tablespoon fresh thyme leaves

For the tahini dressing
juice of 1 lemon
25g coriander leaves
1 tablespoon tahini

Preheat the oven to 180°C/160°C Fan/Gas Mark 4.

Put the nuts and seeds for the dukkah on a baking tray lined with baking parchment. Toast in the oven for 12 minutes. Remove and allow to cool but leave the oven on.

Place the veg on a couple of baking trays in a single layer and coat in the oil, then season with salt and pepper.

Bake for 50–60 minutes, until soft in the middle and caramelised on the outside. Keep your eye on them as they will cook at varying times.

To make the zaatar dressing, put the ingredients into a large jar, secure with the lid and shake to combine. Add the butter beans and shake again. Set aside.

Put all the ingredients for the tahini dressing and 3–4 tablespoons of water into a mini food processor (or use a hand blender) and blitz until creamy.

For the dukkah, add the toasted nuts and seeds and chilli flakes to a mini food processor or spice grinder. Pulse on one-second bursts. Check the consistency after each pulse as you don't want it too finely chopped. Season with salt.

Serve by layering some of the roast veg on a platter, followed by some beans. Dress with tahini dressing and sprinkle with some dukkah. Repeat. Top with lots of fresh herbs.

Bursting with gorgeous summery flavours – roast peppers, tomatoes and aubergine – this panzanella is also a brilliant way to use up slightly squidgy tomatoes, almost-past-their-best peppers and stale bread. The bread works to soak up all the sweet juices from the roasted veg.

Tip: never put tomatoes in the fridge as this will render them tasteless. Always store them in your fruit bowl. They will ripen and develop in flavour there.

Summer in a bowl – panzanella salad

Serves 4

1 large slice day-old sourdough
3 tablespoons pitted green
 olives
3 tablespoons capers
2 spring onions, sliced
 diagonally
½ small cucumber, peeled with
 a vegetable peeler
 into shavings
15g basil leaves, roughly torn
15g mint leaves, roughly torn
50g rocket
2 tablespoons toasted pine nuts
extra virgin olive oil, to drizzle
sea salt flakes and freshly
 ground black pepper

For the roast veg

2 red peppers, deseeded and
 cut into 2cm cubes
1 aubergine, cut into 2cm cubes
250g cherry tomatoes
2–3 tablespoons olive oil

For the dressing

3 tablespoons extra virgin
 olive oil
1 tablespoon apple cider
 vinegar
1 tablespoon pomegranate
 molasses

Preheat the oven to 180°C/160°C Fan/Gas Mark 4.

Firstly roast the veg by adding the peppers and aubergine to a large roasting tray. In a separate tray, add the cherry tomatoes. Drizzle both trays with olive oil and season with salt and pepper. Roast for 35–40 minutes. Set aside.

Now make the dressing by adding all the ingredients to a jar. Replace the lid. Shake to combine. Season to taste.

Toast the bread, then cut into chunky squares. Add the roast peppers and aubergine to a large bowl along with the toast. Pour the dressing over and toss to combine. Add the olives, capers, spring onions, cucumber, herbs, rocket and pine nuts. Toss to combine again.

Serve on a platter and top with the roast tomatoes and more herbs. Finish with a final drizzle of extra virgin olive oil and scatter with a pinch of salt.

Feasting food is my favourite way to eat, with multiple mezze-style dishes laid out on the table for everyone to dig into. This platter is loaded with layered textures and flavours: creamy harissa hummus, crispy-on-the-outside-and-soft-on-the-inside roast cauliflower, silky smooth tahini dressing and zingy zhoug. Serve it with flatbreads, slaw and roast potatoes for a proper feast.

Tip: for a real showstopper you could opt to roast the cauliflower whole for 1–2 hours depending on the size, and then top with the tahini and zhoug.

Loaded Middle Eastern cauliflower platter

Serves 4

1 medium cauliflower, cut into 2.5cm thick steaks including the stalks
1 tablespoon olive oil
1 teaspoon caraway seeds
sea salt flakes and freshly ground black pepper

For the harissa hummus
400g can of chickpeas, rinsed and drained
1 garlic clove
juice of ½ lemon
1 tablespoon tahini
3 tablespoons aquafaba (liquid from a can of chickpeas)
1 tablespoon rose harissa or 1 teaspoon harissa paste
2 tablespoons extra virgin olive oil

For the zhoug
1 teaspoon fennel seeds
1 teaspoon caraway seeds
½ red chilli, deseeded
40g mint leaves
40g coriander, chopped
2 large garlic cloves, roughly chopped
4 tablespoons extra virgin olive oil, plus extra to drizzle
juice of ½ lemon

Preheat the oven to 180°C/160°C Fan/Gas Mark 4.

Add the cauliflower to a large roasting tray. Toss with olive oil, ½ teaspoon of salt and the caraway seeds. Roast in the oven for 20 minutes, then turn. Continue to roast for a further 20 minutes, until the cauliflower steaks are tender and golden brown. Remove from the oven.

Next, add the chickpeas to a food processor or blender with the garlic, lemon juice, tahini, aquafaba, harissa and olive oil, season with salt. Blitz until smooth and creamy (about 2 minutes), and add a little water to loosen if needed. Taste and adjust the seasoning if needed, then blitz again.

Toast the fennel and caraway seeds in a dry frying pan – for a couple of minutes – until fragrant. Allow to cool, then lightly crush using a pestle and mortar. Tip the toasted seeds into a food processor or high-speed blender along with the rest of the ingredients for the zhoug and blitz to a smooth paste. Transfer to a bowl and drizzle with a little extra olive oil.

To make the dressing, add all the ingredients, along with 2 tablespoons of water, to a small bowl and whisk until creamy.

Spread the harissa hummus onto a large serving plate, top with the roasted cauliflower and dollop over the zhoug and tahini dressing. Finish with the toasted seeds and fresh coriander.

For the tahini dressing

1 tablespoon olive oil
juice of ½ lemon
1 tablespoon tahini
1 garlic clove, crushed to a paste

To serve

a mixture of toasted sunflower
    and pumpkin seeds
fresh coriander, torn

AGAINST *the* GRAIN

Here It Is... Where It All Began Store Cupboard Essentials Quick and Easy Transformative Toast Toppers Brunch Big Vegan Breakfasts Curry for Breakfast Radical Curries and Delectable Dals World Flavours Comfort Food Incredible Pastas and Risottos Small Plates A Soup for All Seasons Salad Bliss **Flatbreads and Pizzas 189 Life-changing Pancake Breads 195** Pure Comfort Something Special Tempting Tarts A Little Lighter Devilish Dips and Sauces Life-changing Dressings Pickle and Preserve Like a Pro Plant-based Milks Nut Butters Index About the Author Acknowledgements Here It Is... Where It All Began Store Cupboard Essentials Quick and Easy Transformative Toast Toppers Brunch Big Vegan Breakfasts Curry for Breakfast Radical Curries and Delectable Dals World Flavours Comfort Food Incredible Pastas and Risottos Small Plates A Soup for All Seasons Salad Bliss Flatbreads and Pizzas Life-changing Pancake Breads Pure Comfort Something Special Tempting Tarts A Little Lighter Devilish Dips and Sauces Life-changing Dressings Pickle and Preserve Like a Pro Plant-based Milks Nut Butters Index About the Author Acknowledgements Here It Is... Where It All Began Store Cupboard Essentials Quick and Easy Transformative Toast Toppers Brunch Big Vegan Breakfasts Curry for Breakfast Radical Curries and Delectable Dals World Flavours Comfort Food Incredible Pastas and Risottos Small Plates A Soup for All Seasons Salad Bliss Flatbreads and Pizzas Life-changing Pancake Breads Pure Comfort Something Special Tempting Tarts A Little Lighter Devilish Dips and Sauces Life-changing Dressings Pickle and

I first tasted Turkish pizzas, or pide, when I travelled to Turkey as a teenager. It was my first trip without my parents and an adventure I'll never forget (but that's another story!). These little boat-shaped breads are filled with a mix of spiced aubergine, coconut mint dip, pomegranate seeds and pistachio dukkah, and the flavours are incredibly fresh. This is my classic dough recipe, which is perfect for pitta breads, pizza bases or flatbreads.

Spiced aubergine pide

Makes 4

For the dough
400g plain flour, plus extra to dust
¼ teaspoon sea salt flakes
1 teaspoon fast-active dried yeast
1 teaspoon sugar
2 tablespoons olive oil, plus extra to grease
320ml lukewarm water

For the aubergine filling
1 onion, finely chopped
1 tablespoon olive oil
2 garlic cloves, finely chopped
1 teaspoon cumin seeds
½ teaspoon smoked paprika
½ teaspoon ground cinnamon
½ teaspoon dried chilli flakes
1 medium aubergine, cut into 1cm cubes
3 tomatoes, chopped
½ teaspoon sea salt flakes
a pinch of ground sumac
a big handful of mint, roughly chopped

For the coconut mint dip
3 tablespoons coconut yoghurt
juice of ½ lemon
1 tablespoon olive oil
1 garlic clove, peeled and grated
4 tablespoons chopped fresh mint
a big pinch of sea salt flakes

For the topping
pistachio dukkah (page 252)
2 tablespoons pomegranate seeds
a handful of fresh mint

First, make the dough. Add the flour and salt to a large bowl and mix well.

In a small bowl, combine the yeast, sugar, olive oil and warm water, and leave to sit for a minute or so until frothy.

Create a hole in the middle of the flour mixture and gradually add the yeast mixture, using your hands to combine and form a dough. Tip the dough onto a floured chopping board. Knead for a few minutes until the dough becomes springy, then transfer into a bowl greased with oil. Cover with a damp cloth for about 1–1½ hours, until the dough has doubled in size.

While the dough is rising, make the filling. Add the onion to a large pan with the olive oil and sauté over a low heat for 10 minutes. Add in the garlic and spices, and fry for a further few minutes. Now add in the aubergine, and stir-fry over a low heat for a minute more. Add the chopped tomatoes, then cover the pan and cook, stirring occasionally, for 15 minutes. Next, add in the salt, sumac and chopped mint, and stir to combine. Remove from the heat and set aside.

For the coconut mint dip, put all the ingredients into a jar, secure with the lid and shake to combine. Add a little water to loosen if desired.

Preheat the oven to 200°C/180°C Fan/Gas Mark 6. Lightly oil a large baking tray.

Transfer the dough back onto the floured chopping board and knead again for a minute to knock back. Divide the dough into quarters, then roll out into long oval shapes. Pinch the dough at each end so as to make a boat shape. Spoon the aubergine filling onto the central part of each pide, leaving a border of around 1.5cm. Then fold the edges of the dough up to overlap the filling a little.

Carefully transfer each pide onto the oiled baking tray. Bake for 15 minutes, until the crust is cooked and a little golden. Remove from the oven and allow to cool a little. Serve the pide topped with the coconut mint dip, dukkah, pomegranate seeds and fresh mint leaves.

I'm not sure I can contain my excitement about this recipe – I mean it's a curry pizza! Chunky coconut chickpea curry on a fluffy griddled flatbread pizza base with the creamiest coconut mint dip – it really is incredibly delicious. The same principle as curry with chapatis but somehow more decadent in pizza form. The pizza is a great pairing with my Tomato Curry on page 82.

Coconut chana masala pizza *with* mint yoghurt

Serves 2

freshly chopped coriander, to serve
extra virgin olive oil, to serve
sea salt flakes and freshly ground black pepper

For the pizza dough
200g spelt flour (or 100g spelt and 100g strong white flour), plus extra for dusting
¼ teaspoon sea salt flakes
1 teaspoon dried yeast
1 teaspoon sugar
2 tablespoons olive oil, plus extra to grease
175ml lukewarm water

For the chana masala curry
2 tablespoons olive oil
1 teaspoon black mustard seeds
1 teaspoon cumin seeds
1 teaspoon ground coriander
½ teaspoon dried chilli flakes
1 teaspoon ground turmeric
1 onion, roughly chopped
2 garlic cloves, sliced
a thumb-sized piece of ginger, peeled and finely grated
6 ripe tomatoes, chopped
2 tablespoons unsweetened desiccated coconut

Make the dough. Add the flour and salt to a large bowl and mix well.

In a small bowl, mix together the yeast, sugar and olive oil with the lukewarm water and leave for 5 minutes to activate.

Create a hole in the middle of the flour mixture and gradually add the liquid, mixing until you have a dough. Tip the dough onto a well-floured chopping board. Knead for a few minutes, adding a little more flour if needed, until the dough is soft and springy.

Transfer the dough into an oiled bowl and cover with a clean damp cloth. Leave to sit for 1–1½ hours, or until the dough has doubled in size. Transfer the dough back onto the floured board and knead again to knock back.

For the curry, heat the oil in a large frying pan over a medium heat. Add in the mustard seeds. When they start to pop, add in the cumin seeds, coriander, chilli flakes and turmeric. Stir for a few seconds, then add in the onion. Fry for 8–10 minutes, until soft and browning. Add in the garlic and ginger and stir for another 1 minute, then add in the chopped tomatoes and desiccated coconut. Cover the pan with a lid and cook for a further 5–6 minutes, stirring occasionally, then add in the chickpeas. Simmer for 5 minutes. Season with salt and pepper to taste and stir in the coconut yoghurt.

Place all the ingredients for the mint dip in a jar, secure with a lid and shake to combine.

Preheat a griddle pan over a medium-high heat.

240g cooked or canned
    chickpeas, rinsed and drained
3 tablespoons coconut yoghurt
    or plant-based milk of choice

For the mint dip
4 tablespoons coconut yoghurt
1 garlic clove, crushed
2 tablespoons lemon juice
3 tablespoons chopped
    fresh mint

Meanwhile, cut the dough into two portions and roll out on a floured surface to around 20cm in diameter. Brush with oil and place on the preheated griddle pan. Cook for a couple of minutes on each side until charred on the outside and fluffy in the middle. Repeat with the remaining pizza base. Top each pizza with the curry, coriander and a drizzle of extra virgin olive oil. Serve the mint dip on the side.

Pizzas are another little obsession of mine. I've got so many different pizza recipes on my blog it's actually quite funny. I particularly love these though – mini flatbread pizzas with pesto and roast tomatoes. It's an amazing flavour combination.

For the pizza bases, you can choose to go with rye; spelt flour that gives a nutty and firmer crust; a 50-50 mix of spelt and plain white flour – my favourite for a nutty and fluffy texture; or just plain white flour for a classic flatbread.

Pesto *and* roast tomato mini rye flatbread pizza

Makes 8 mini pizzas or 4 large

250g cherry tomatoes
1 tablespoon olive oil
spinach and pine nut pesto (page 250)
a handful of rocket
dried chilli flakes
a drizzle of extra virgin olive oil
sea salt flakes

For the base

200g flour of choice (see introduction), plus extra for dusting
1 teaspoon baking powder
100g coconut yoghurt or plant-based yoghurt of choice

Preheat the oven to 180°C/160°C Fan/Gas Mark 4.

Add the cherry tomatoes and olive oil to a large baking tray and toss to coat. Roast for 30 minutes or until soft and browning a little. Set aside.

In a large bowl, add the flour, baking powder and a pinch of salt. Stir to combine. Now add the yoghurt and 75ml of water, mix thoroughly to combine and then transfer to a floured surface. Knead for a few minutes until you get a rough springy dough. Pop it back in the bowl and cover with a damp tea towel. Leave to rest for 15 minutes.

Preheat a large griddle pan or frying pan over a medium-high heat. Divide the dough into eight portions (alternatively, divide into four portions if you want to make large pizzas), then roll out on a floured surface to the thickness of a coin.

Pop a flatbread on the griddle pan and allow to cook and char for 2 minutes, then flip to char on the other side. Remove and keep warm on a plate, and cover with a clean tea towel. Repeat with the remaining flatbreads.

Top with the pesto, roasted cherry tomatoes, rocket, chilli flakes, sea salt and a slick of extra virgin olive oil if you like.

variation

Add some cashew 'parmesan' (page 137) as a topping option to your flatbread pizzas.

Pancake breads are one of the easiest ways of whipping up delicious – slightly squidgy – flatbreads in minutes. I've been making them for years with various combinations of flours and seasonings. Some of my favourites appear in the book, one being this farinata, an Italian chickpea flour and olive oil pancake.

Farinata is super easy to make, delicious, gluten free and contains plant-based protein. I always keep a big bag of gram (chickpea) flour in the store cupboard and make it a few times a week.

Farinata *with* kale pesto

Serves 2–4

150g gram (chickpea) flour
½ teaspoon baking powder
1 tablespoon extra virgin olive oil
2 tablespoons olive oil
1 thyme sprig, leaves picked
sea salt flakes and freshly ground black pepper

For the kale pesto
90g kale, tough stalks removed
50g walnuts
25g basil leaves
2 tablespoons olive oil
grated zest of 1 lemon and juice of ½ lemon
2 garlic cloves
3 tablespoons nutritional yeast flakes

Mix the chickpea flour, baking powder and 1 teaspoon of salt in a large bowl, then add 300ml of cold water and the extra virgin olive oil, and whisk well to get rid of the lumps. Let the mixture rest for 1 hour.

Preheat the oven to 180°C/160°C Fan/Gas Mark 4.

Line a 20 x 30cm baking tray, add 1 tablespoon of the olive oil and tilt the tray to evenly distribute the oil over the base. Pour in the farinata mixture, then sprinkle with the fresh thyme and sea salt flakes.

Bake for 10–12 minutes, until set in the middle. Remove from the oven and drizzle with a little more extra virgin olive oil and give it a good grind of black pepper.

While the farinata is cooking, make the pesto. Add all the ingredients to a food processor or high-speed blender along with 75ml of water and blitz to a paste. Season to taste.

Dollop generous amounts of pesto on to the farinata, and cut into pieces to serve.

variation

Other topping options include hummus, caponata or olive tapenade.

Staffordshire oatcakes, if you don't know, are a type of squidgy pancake bread made from oat flour. They're absolutely delicious. I was introduced to them by my then-boyfriend in Lichfield many years ago and fell a bit in love with them.

They are very easy to make. Here, I've topped them with crispy kale and roast tomatoes but as a quick treat you could spread them with tomato paste, top with plant-based cheese and then pop under the grill. Delicious!

Staffordshire oatcakes
with roast balsamic tomatoes *and* crispy kale

Makes 4 pancakes

For the Staffordshire oatcakes
100g plain or spelt flour
100g oat flour (or blitz oats in a food processor or high-speed blender)
½ teaspoon sea salt flakes
1 teaspoon fast-action yeast
½ teaspoon bicarbonate of soda
½ teaspoon caster sugar
1 teaspoon apple cider vinegar
125ml almond milk or plant-based milk of choice

For the roast balsamic tomatoes
250g cherry tomatoes
olive oil, for drizzling
½ teaspoon balsamic vinegar
sea salt flakes

For the crispy kale
1 tablespoon olive oil
70g kale, tough stalks removed
sea salt flakes and freshly ground black pepper

To make the batter, mix the dry ingredients in a large bowl. Add the vinegar, milk and 300ml of water. Mix well and allow to sit, uncovered, for at least 1 hour. The mix will bubble and rise.

Preheat the oven to 180°C/160°C Fan/Gas Mark 4.

Put the tomatoes on a baking tray and drizzle with olive oil and balsamic vinegar. Sprinkle with a pinch of salt and toss. Roast for 25 minutes. Set aside.

Heat the oil in a frying pan over a medium heat. Add the kale and fry for a few minutes, until crispy. Season well with salt and pepper. Set aside.

To cook the oatcakes, heat a non-stick pan over a medium heat. Spoon a ladleful of the batter into the pan, tilting the pan slightly to distribute the batter all over the base. (Alternatively, use the ladle to distribute the batter in a circular motion.) Allow to cook for 1–2 minutes, until the oatcake begins to come away at the edges of the pan and is bubbling in the middle. Carefully flip over and cook on the other side for a minute or so. Remove to a plate and keep warm under a clean tea towel. Repeat with the remaining batter.

To serve, top the oatcakes with the roast tomatoes and crispy kale.

I first started making soda bread as a teenager in cooking class at school, and have never stopped. If you haven't made it before you'll be amazed just how easy it is to have fresh bread in under 40 minutes.

You can use most flours here but I love spelt as it makes a gorgeously dense and nutty loaf. The soda bread is just heavenly paired with nut butter and warm berry compote.

Spelt soda bread
with nut butter *and*
warm blackberries

Makes 1 loaf

350g wholemeal spelt flour, plus extra to dust
3 teaspoons caraway seeds
1 teaspoon sea salt flakes
2 tablespoons chopped hazelnuts
1 teaspoon bicarbonate of soda
250ml almond milk or plant-based milk of choice
75g coconut yoghurt or plant-based yoghurt of choice
1 tablespoon apple cider vinegar
a handful of oats, to sprinkle

For the blackberry compote
150g blackberries
a splash of maple syrup
a squeeze of lemon juice

To serve
homemade nut butter (page 270) (I use peanut butter)
coconut yoghurt
fresh thyme or mint leaves

Preheat the oven to 200°C/180°C Fan/Gas Mark 6.

Mix all the dry ingredients together thoroughly in a large bowl. Add the milk, yoghurt and vinegar, and stir to combine; the mixture should come together into a dough. Form into a ball and place on a floured baking tray, and then cut a deep cross in the centre. Sprinkle some oats on the top. Now transfer the bread to the preheated oven and bake for 35–40 minutes.

Remove from the oven and allow to cool a little.

While the bread is baking, put the ingredients for the compote into a saucepan. Place over a medium-high heat until the berries have broken down a little.

Once the bread has cooled, slice and either toast or just smear with some peanut butter, coconut yoghurt, blackberry compote and fresh herbs.

Can't Believe It's Vegan
DESSERTS

Here It Is... Where It All Began Store Cupboard Essentials
Quick and Easy Transformative Toast Toppers Brunch Big
Vegan Breakfasts Curry for Breakfast Radical Curries and
Delectable Dals World Flavours Comfort Food Incredible
Pastas and Risottos Small Plates A Soup for All Seasons
Salad Bliss Flatbreads and Pizzas Life-changing Pancake
Breads **Pure Comfort 206 Something Special 215
Tempting Tarts 226 A Little Lighter 234** Devilish
Dips and Sauces Life-changing Dressings Pickle and Preserve
Like a Pro Plant-based Milks Nut Butters Index About the
Author Acknowledgements Here It Is... Where It All Began
Store Cupboard Essentials Quick and Easy Transformative
Toast Toppers Brunch Big Vegan Breakfasts Curry for
Breakfast Radical Curries and Delectable Dals World Flavours
Comfort Food Incredible Pastas and Risottos Small Plates
A Soup for All Seasons Salad Bliss Flatbreads and Pizzas
Life-changing Pancake Breads Pure Comfort Something
Special Tempting Tarts A Little Lighter Devilish Dips and
Sauces Life-changing Dressings Pickle and Preserve Like a
Pro Plant-based Milks Nut Butters Index About the Author
Acknowledgements Here It Is... Where It All Began Store
Cupboard Essentials Quick and Easy Transformative Toast
Toppers Brunch Big Vegan Breakfasts Curry for Breakfast
Radical Curries and Delectable Dals World Flavours Comfort
Food Incredible Pastas and Risottos Small Plates A Soup for
All Seasons Salad Bliss Flatbreads and Pizzas Life-changing
Pancake Breads Pure Comfort Something Special Tempting
Tarts A Little Lighter Devilish Dips and Sauces Life-changing

Banana and jam crumble was my absolute favourite primary school pudding so I couldn't resist coming up with my own version. I can remember the pudding so vividly I feel like I can taste it now ... gooey banana, sweet jam and crunchy crumble topping.

I bring you a more grown-up version here – caramelised banana and sticky dates, the crunchiest peanut butter crumble topping and cardamom custard. I hope you love this as much as I do.

On the off chance this delicious crumble isn't polished off straight away, it's just as delicious eaten for breakfast with a big dollop of coconut yoghurt.

Tip: the cardamom custard is absolutely fantastic paired with my Cherry Almond Tart (page 226).

Caramelised banana *and* peanut butter crumble
with
cardamom custard

Serves 8–10

100g ground almonds
50g jumbo oats
3 tablespoons rice flour
2 tablespoons ground flaxseeds
3 tablespoons sunflower seeds
1 teaspoon ground allspice
1 teaspoon ground cinnamon
½ teaspoon ground cardamom
a pinch of ground nutmeg
½ teaspoon sea salt flakes
1 teaspoon baking powder
6 tablespoons good-quality
 peanut butter
6 tablespoons maple syrup
1 teaspoon almond extract
1 teaspoon vanilla extract

For the caramelised
bananas
2 tablespoons coconut oil
6 ripe bananas, sliced in half
 lengthways

Preheat the oven to 180°C/160°C Fan/Gas Mark 4.

First caramelise the bananas. Melt the coconut oil in a large frying pan, then add in half the sliced bananas (depending on how large your pan is, you might want to do this step in batches).

Add a splash of maple syrup and allow the bananas to caramelise. Turn over to caramelise the other side. Remove, scraping the pan for any sticky caramelised bits, into a bowl and set aside. Repeat the process with the remaining bananas.

Add the bananas to a large baking dish. Pour the milk over the top, sprinkle over the desiccated coconut and scatter over the dates.

For the crumble, mix the dry ingredients together in a bowl. In a separate small bowl, mix together the peanut butter, maple syrup, almond and vanilla extracts. Add this wet mixture to the dry mixture and stir thoroughly to bring the ingredients together, then use your hands to form a crumbly mix.

Spread the crumble topping over the bananas and bake for 25–30 minutes, until golden. Remove from the oven and allow to cool a little.

a splash of maple syrup

400ml coconut milk

2 tablespoons desiccated
coconut

6 pitted medjool dates,
roughly chopped

For the cardamom custard

500ml almond milk or other
plant-based milk of choice

1–2 tablespoons maple syrup

1 teaspoon ground cardamom

1 teaspoon vanilla extract

2 tablespoons cornflour, stirred
with 6 tablespoons water to
make a paste

Meanwhile, make the custard by adding the almond milk, maple syrup, ground cardamom and vanilla extract to a small saucepan. Place over a medium-high heat, bring to the boil, then reduce the heat to medium. Add in the cornflour-water paste and cook, stirring continuously, until thickened.

Serve the crumble with the custard poured over the top.

One of my favourite childhood cakes was the dense and sticky slab of Jamaican ginger cake, This is my version, with chestnut and beautiful warming spices, and topped with peanut butter frosting. All you need to do is blitz the ingredients in your food processor, bake and top with frosting – viola! It's also a gluten-free delight.

Ginger *and* chestnut cake *with* peanut butter frosting

Makes 1 x 20cm cake

2 tablespoons coconut oil, plus
   extra for greasing
150g buckwheat flour
90g ground almonds
2 tablespoons ground flaxseeds
1½ teaspoons baking powder
½ teaspoon bicarbonate of soda
½ teaspoon sea salt flakes
175g cooked chestnuts
375ml full-fat coconut milk
3 tablespoons blackstrap
   molasses
100g medjool dates, pitted
2 tablespoons maple syrup
1 tablespoon vanilla extract
20g ground ginger
2 teaspoons ground cinnamon
½ teaspoon ground cloves

For the peanut butter frosting

6 tablespoons peanut butter
1 teaspoon vanilla extract
4 tablespoons coconut cream
   or coconut yoghurt
3 tablespoons maple syrup
a pinch of sea salt flakes

Preheat the oven to 180°C/160°C Fan/Gas Mark 4. Grease a 20cm cake tin with coconut oil.

Add all the ingredients for the cake to a food processor or high-speed blender and blitz to form a smooth batter. Spoon the batter into the prepared tin and bake for 40 minutes, or until a skewer inserted into the middle comes out clean.

Meanwhile make the frosting. Mix all the ingredients in a bowl until well combined. Pop in the fridge to firm up for 20 minutes.

When the cake is done, remove and allow to cool in the tin for 10–15 minutes before turning out onto a wire rack to cool.

Once the cake has cooled completely, use a spatula to smooth the frosting over the top of the cake.

While there is a plethora of sticky bun recipes out there, I wanted to create an extra sticky and indulgent version that was altogether made from (mostly) natural and wholesome ingredients, so I came up with this recipe. The soft buns swirled with salted date caramel and topped with pecans look gorgeous and taste incredible.

Salted date *and* salted caramel pecan buns

Makes 9

For the dough
200g plain flour, plus extra
  for dusting
200g wholemeal flour
¼ teaspoon sea salt flakes
2 teaspoons fast-action yeast
3 teaspoons caster sugar
2 tablespoons olive oil
275ml lukewarm water
75ml plant-based milk of
  choice, at room temperature

For the salted caramel date filling
110g medjool dates, pitted
3 tablespoons peanut butter or
  nut butter of choice
75ml almond milk or plant-
  based milk of choice
1 tablespoon coconut oil
½ teaspoon sea salt flakes

For the topping
120g pecans, roughly chopped
2 tablespoons coconut oil, plus
  extra for greasing
50ml plant-based milk of choice
80ml maple syrup
a pinch of sea salt flakes

Firstly make the dough. Combine the flours with the salt in a large bowl.

In a separate bowl, mix the yeast, sugar, olive oil, lukewarm water and milk and leave for a minute or so. Create a hole in the middle of the dry ingredients and gradually add the wet ingredients. Use a wooden spoon to bring the mixture together, then use clean hands to knead to form a wet dough. Tip the dough onto a floured surface. Knead until the dough is smooth and springy, about 5 minutes. Transfer back to the bowl, cover with a damp tea towel and leave to sit for about 1 hour. The dough should have doubled in size.

Meanwhile, make the caramel filling. Place the ingredients for the filling into a food processor or high-speed blender and blitz until smooth and creamy – it will be a few minutes before all the dates are thoroughly blended in. Set aside 2 tablespoons of the mixture for the topping.

Grease a 23cm round baking dish or tin with coconut oil.

Spread the pecans over the base of the prepared dish or tin. In a saucepan, over a medium heat, melt together the coconut oil, milk, 50ml of maple syrup, salt and the reserved 2 tablespoons of the filling mixture. Bring to the boil and cook over s medium heat for 1 minute; now very carefully pour over the pecans into the dish.

Put the dough on a floured surface and knead to knock back. Roll your dough out on the floured surface into a 35cm x 25cm rectangle and spread with the date caramel. Roll the dough starting from the longest edge to form a scroll, then cut it into nine even portions.

Arrange the buns on top of the caramel and pecans in the dish, making sure they are evenly spaced. Cover with a tea towel and allow to prove for 40 minutes. Meanwhile, preheat the oven to 160°C/140°C Fan/Gas Mark 3.

Bake the buns for 35–40 minutes. Remove from oven and allow to cool for 10 minutes before inverting onto a board and drizzling with the extra maple syrup.

I'm quite proud of this delicious baked cheesecake. It's the result of playing around with many topping ingredients. I've made it countless times for my friends who are devoted taste-testers (for this and many other recipes in the book).

If you read the ingredients list you may be a bit sceptical, but trust me they work together to create a fantastic texture and flavour reminiscent of a classic cheesecake. And topped with oozing warm berries, it's wonderful.

Baked tahini coconut cheesecake
with ginger pecan crust *and* warm berries

Makes 1 x 25cm cake

2 tablespoons cornflour
175g cashews, soaked in
    boiling water for 15 minutes
    (alternatively soak in water
    for 4 hours), drained
400g can of chickpeas, rinsed
    and drained
grated zest and juice of 1 lemon
3 teaspoons vanilla extract
6 tablespoons agave or
    maple syrup
6 tablespoons tahini
250g coconut yoghurt
½ teaspoon sea salt flakes
1 tablespoon apple cider vinegar
fresh mint leaves, to garnish

For the ginger pecan base
200g pecans
2 teaspoons ground ginger
12 medjool dates, pitted
2 tablespoons buckwheat groats
a pinch of sea salt flakes

For the berries
75g blueberries
75g blackberries
a splash of maple syrup

Preheat the oven to 180°C/160°C Fan/Gas Mark 4. Grease a 25cm loose-bottomed cake tin and line the sides with baking parchment.

Make the base. Add the ingredients to a food processor or high-speed blender and blitz to form a crumbly yet sticky mixture. Tip into the prepared tin and press the mixture evenly and firmly over the base.

To make the filling, firstly mix the cornflour with 2 tablespoons of water in a small bowl.

Add the cornflour-water mix and all the remaining ingredients to a food processor or high-speed blender and blitz until very smooth and creamy. Spoon over the base and out to the edges.

Bake for 40 minutes or until firm at the sides and just about set in the middle with just a bit of a wobble. Allow the cake to cool before transferring it to the fridge overnight.

When you're just about ready to serve, add the berries and maple syrup to a small saucepan and place over a low heat until the berries have broken down a little.

Spoon the berries over the cheesecake. Sprinkle with fresh mint.

This dessert combines some of my favourite things: beautiful ripe cherries, chocolate and coffee. I'm definitely one to enjoy an espresso after dinner, and if it can be incorporated into dessert then all the better. These rich and decadent ganache pots are the perfect size, not too big to be cloying but large enough to give that chocolate hit with the little gooey cherries nestled inside.

Cherry chocolate ganache espresso pots

Serves 4

100g fresh cherries, pitted and chopped in half
2½ tablespoons maple syrup
100g good-quality vegan chocolate
250ml coconut cream
2 tablespoons coconut oil
½ teaspoon vanilla extract
2 tablespoons raw cacao
1–2 teaspoons espresso powder

Firstly, add the cherries to a saucepan with ½ tablespoon of maple syrup and a splash of water. Place over a medium heat for a few minutes until the cherries have softened a little. Set aside.

Now break up the chocolate into bite-sized pieces and add to a large bowl.

Heat the coconut cream, coconut oil, remaining 2 tablespoons of maple syrup and the vanilla in a saucepan over a low heat, stirring constantly, until almost boiling. Take the pan off the heat and pour the mixture over the chocolate in the bowl. Leave to sit for a few minutes to allow the chocolate to melt.

Fold the raw cacao and espresso powder into the chocolate mixture gently – just until everything is combined. Now fold in the cherries.

Spoon the mixture into four small glasses or espresso cups then pop in the fridge to firm up – around 4 hours or overnight.

These little truffles are truly addictive so be warned. My sister Ems demands that they are brought with me – ideally on all visits.

The key ingredient and the thing that makes them creamy is the avocado. When blended together with the other ingredients – the best quality vegan chocolate, raw cacao, coconut oil and coconut honey or maple syrup – you get this incredibly smooth truffle. The taste is so densely rich and dark – what's not to love?

Chocolate avocado truffles

Makes 20

1 ripe avocado
4 tablespoons raw cacao
2 tablespoons coconut honey
   or maple syrup
a pinch of sea salt flakes
2 tablespoons coconut oil
80g good-quality vegan
   chocolate, broken into
   small pieces
½ teaspoon vanilla extract

To make the truffles, peel and destone the avocado and add the flesh to a food processor or high-speed blender along with 3 tablespoons of the raw cacao, honey and sea salt flakes. Blitz until very smooth and creamy.

In a saucepan, and over a low heat, very gently melt the coconut oil and chocolate, then add this to the food processor. Add the vanilla extract then pulse to combine everything.

Transfer the mix to a lidded container and then pop into the fridge for a couple of hours to firm up so that the truffles can be easily rolled.

To shape the truffles, scoop out bite-sized pieces of the mixture and roll into balls. Roll the balls in the remaining tablespoon of cacao. Put in a container or on a plate covered in clingfilm and chill in the fridge where they will keep for up to a few days.

These truffles can also be frozen and then just taken out when you want a little bite.

nutty truffles variation

Scoop out bite-sized pieces of the truffle mixture and roll into balls. Flatten a ball with your palm and insert a hazelnut into the centre. Fold the mixture around the nut, then roll to make a ball. Repeat with the remaining mixture and coat with chopped hazelnuts.

This brownie cake is a much-loved recipe from my blog. Probably because it has just the right amount of dense chocolatey texture, enough sweetness from the dates and a gorgeous almond flavour.

The secret ingredient? Chestnuts. They give the brownie an amazing depth of flavour. I like to top my cake with a simple cashew cream and whatever berries are in season.

Flourless chocolate, almond *and* chestnut brownie cake

Makes 1 x 20cm cake

100g good-quality vegan
    chocolate, broken up
    into pieces
2 tablespoons coconut
    oil, melted
175g cooked chestnuts
9 medjool dates, pitted
100g ground almonds
2 tablespoons raw
    cacao powder
½ teaspoon baking powder
½ teaspoon almond extract
1 tablespoon vanilla extract
a pinch of sea salt flakes
35g coconut sugar
berries of choice, for
    the topping

For the cashew cream

200g cashews, soaked in water
    for 10 minutes
grated zest and juice of 1 lemon
2 tablespoons maple syrup
½ tablespoon vanilla extract
a pinch of sea salt flakes

Preheat the oven to 180°C/160°C Fan/Gas Mark 4. Line a 20cm loose-bottomed cake tin with baking parchment.

Melt the chocolate in a heatproof bowl set over a pan of simmering water (do not let the bowl touch the water). Put the coconut oil and chestnuts in a food processor or high-speed blender and blitz for 1–2 minutes. Add in the dates and blitz again. Finally, add the melted chocolate, ground almonds, cacao, baking powder, almond and vanilla extracts, salt and coconut sugar, and blitz until everything is well combined (note, the batter is super thick).

Spoon the batter into the prepared cake tin and use wet hands to press the mix in. Bake for 25 minutes, until the edges are beginning to get a little brown. The cake will be slightly gooey in the middle but it will set completely once cooled.

To make the cashew cream, drain the cashews and pop all the ingredients into a food processor or high-speed blender and blitz until smooth and creamy. Add a splash or two of water if the consistency is a little thick.

When the cake is done, remove from the oven and allow to cool for 15 minutes in the tin. After this time, carefully turn out onto a wire rack and leave to cool completely. Spread the top with cashew cream and scatter with berries to serve.

optional variation

To create a fruitcake version, stir 50g of dried mixed fruit into the batter just before spooning the mixture into the cake tin.

There are two Italian desserts that I absolutely love – afogatto and tiramisu. Unfortunately they are rarely vegan so I wanted to take my favourite elements and create a delicious dairy-free reimagining.

This is my vegan 'tiramisu'. Without the sponge it's more of a sundae in four layers. The base is an incredible crunchy crumble. This is topped with a silky coffee cream, a coconut cream and finally a chocolate syrup. I think it captures the spirit and tastes amazing.

Easy tiramisu pots

Makes 6

For the coconut cream
400g coconut cream
1 tablespoon maple syrup
½ teaspoon vanilla extract

For the chocolate crumble layer
200g walnuts, toasted
8 medjool dates, pitted
1 teaspoon espresso powder
1 teaspoon vanilla extract
1 tablespoon raw cacao
2 tablespoons cacao nibs
a pinch of sea salt flakes

For the coffee cream
350g silken tofu
15g espresso powder brewed in
   60ml hot water, cooled
3 tablespoons maple syrup
1 teaspoon vanilla extract

For the chocolate syrup
2 tablespoons coconut oil
2 tablespoons raw cacao
2 tablespoons maple syrup
1 teaspoon espresso powder
1 teaspoon vanilla extract

Firstly make the coconut cream. Add all the ingredients to a food processor or high-speed blender and blitz until smooth and fluffy. Don't over-blitz as you will lose the fluffiness. Transfer to a bowl and pop in the fridge to firm up. Wash and dry the food processor bowl.

Now make the crumble layer by blitzing all the ingredients to a chunky crumble in the food processor or high-speed blender. Set aside.

For the coffee cream, add all the ingredients to the food processor or high-speed blender and blitz until very smooth and creamy. Set aside.

To make the chocolate syrup, set a heatproof bowl over a pan of boiling water (make sure the water doesn't touch the base of the bowl). Add the ingredients for the syrup to the bowl and heat gently for 2–3 minutes until melted and combined.

Now you can start layering. Use six 200ml capacity glasses and layer in the crumble followed by the coffee cream, then the coconut cream. Finish with the chocolate syrup. Repeat. These tiramisu pots can be eaten immediately or kept in the fridge overnight and served cold.

This smooth and creamy chocolate ganache tart is a firm favourite on my blog. Chocolate lovers, this one is for you. I'm not exaggerating when I say that I think this is the best chocolate dessert I've ever made: the crispy nutty base combined with the rich and intense chocolatey ganache filling is just heavenly.

I've given a few flavour options and suggested toppings. Choose as you wish!

The best chocolate ganache tart

Makes 1 x 23cm tart

100g best-quality vegan chocolate
250ml coconut cream
2 tablespoons coconut oil
2 tablespoons maple syrup
½ teaspoon vanilla extract
1 tablespoon raw cacao

Flavour options
1 tablespoon orange blossom extract
1 tablespoon espresso powder
1 teaspoon almond extract
1 teaspoon mint extract

For the base
150g walnuts
10 medjool dates, pitted
2 tablespoons raw cacao
2 tablespoons buckwheat groats
a pinch of sea salt flakes

To serve (choose from any of the below)
raspberry compote (page 38)
berries of choice
vegan ice cream
whipped coconut cream (page 227)

Preheat the oven to 200°C/180°C Fan/Gas Mark 6.

Spread the walnuts on a baking tray and toast in the oven for 5–6 minutes, until a shade darker. Remove and allow to cool.

Next, break up the chocolate and add to a large bowl.

Heat the coconut cream, coconut oil, maple syrup and vanilla in a saucepan, stirring constantly, until just before boiling point.

Pour the mixture over the chocolate and leave for a few minutes to allow the chocolate to melt. Fold in the cacao and one of the flavour options (or another of your choice), and stir gently so that everything is combined. Pop in the fridge while you make the base.

To make the base, blitz the toasted walnuts in your food processor until you get a crumb-like consistency. Add in the dates, cacao, buckwheat and salt, and blend again until everything combines. The mixture should stick together between your fingers. Add the mixture to a 23cm tart tin and, using your hands, press down firmly to form an even base and sides.

Remove the ganache from the fridge and pour onto the base. Transfer back to your fridge and allow to set for at least 2–3 hours. Serve with any or a combination of the suggestions given here.

variations

Try the below flavour combos for some perfect pairings:
Chocolate orange blossom tart served with orange slices and coconut cream.
Chocolate mint tart served with fresh mint leaves and vegan ice cream.

Back to my love of the Bakewell tart here – I can't get enough of its almondy deliciousness. My version has a nutty base and a rich and gooey frangipane filling, sweet cherries and a layer of cherry jam. Oh my goodness, it's good. And served with whipped coconut cream – it's tart heaven.

Cherry almond tart
with
whipped cream

Makes 1 x 23cm tart

coconut oil, to grease
2 tablespoons ground flaxseeds
75g vegan butter or spread
75g coconut sugar, plus
   2 teaspoons
3 teaspoons almond extract
150g ground almonds
2 tablespoons gluten-free flour
   or plain flour
1 teaspoon baking powder
finely grated zest of 1 lemon
100g fresh or frozen pitted
   cherries (if frozen, defrosted),
   halved, plus 40g extra to top
3–4 tablespoons cherry jam
a handful of flaked almonds,
   to sprinkle
icing sugar, to dust (optional)

For the base

2 tablespoons ground flaxseeds
50g ground almonds
100g gluten-free flour or
   plain flour
50g buckwheat flour
½ teaspoon sea salt flakes
2 teaspoons coconut sugar
2 tablespoons rapeseed oil
3 tablespoons almond milk or
   plant-based milk of choice

Preheat the oven to 180°C/160°C Fan/Gas Mark 4. Grease a 23cm round tart tin with a removable base with a little coconut oil.

Make the flax 'egg' for the base by mixing the ground flaxseeds with 6 tablespoons of water in a small bowl. Set aside for 10 minutes to thicken.

To make the base, combine the ground almonds, flours, salt and sugar in a large bowl. Add in the oil, almond milk and flax 'egg'. Mix thoroughly to form a thick batter.

Transfer the mixture to the prepared tin and use your fingers to press it evenly along the bottom and up the sides. Poke a few holes with a fork across the base.

Bake in the oven for 10 minutes, until the pastry has dried out and there is no trace of moisture. Remove from the oven and allow to cool a little.

Make up the remaining flax 'egg' by mixing the remaining 2 tablespoons of ground flaxseeds with 6 tablespoons of water in a small bowl. Set aside and allow to thicken for 10 minutes.

Using a hand-held mixer or whisk, cream together the butter, 75g of coconut sugar and the almond extract. Stir in the flax 'egg'.

In a large bowl, mix the ground almonds, flour and baking powder. Transfer the butter mix to the dry ingredients. Mix together to combine thoroughly, then stir in the lemon zest.

Heat the cherries in a saucepan with the 2 teaspoons of sugar, over a low heat, just until softened a little. Take off the heat and set aside.

Layer the jam across the bottom of the tart, followed by the softened cherries. Now spoon the frangipane filling over the top. Top with extra

For the whipped coconut cream

175g coconut cream
2 tablespoons drinking coconut milk
1 tablespoon maple syrup
½ teaspoon vanilla extract

cherries, pressing them down a little into the frangipane. Sprinkle with flaked almonds.

Bake for 45–50 minutes until the filling is set.

To make the coconut cream, add all ingredients to a food processor or high-speed blender and blitz until smooth and fluffy (if using a blender, make sure to do this on low). Don't over-blitz as you want the cream to be light and fluffy. Transfer to a tub then pop in the fridge to firm up.

Remove the tart from the oven and allow to cool a little before removing carefully from the tin and transferring to a wire rack to cool completely. Sift over some icing sugar if you want to make it look prettier.

Serve with the whipped coconut cream.

Nothing says summer quite like a huge slice of lemon tart. Lemon curd was my favourite spread when I was a little girl, and I used to love it on toast. I loved it so much I used to take cold toast and lemon curd to school for lunch, and I also used to sandwich it between pancakes.

To this tart, I've added fresh thyme for a more grown-up version but it still delivers all that creamy lemon curd deliciousness, and paired with the crispy nutty base it's perfect. This is my mum's favourite – and mums know best.

Liberating lemon curd *and* thyme tart

Makes 1 x 20cm tart

For the tart base
2 tablespoons ground flaxseeds
50g ground almonds
75g gluten-free oat flour
60g buckwheat flour
½ teaspoon sea salt flakes
1 teaspoon coconut sugar
1½ tablespoons neutral oil
 such as rapeseed oil, plus
 extra for greasing
3 tablespoons almond milk

For the filling
3 tablespoons cornflour
finely grated zest of 4 unwaxed
 lemons and juice of 3 lemons
250ml coconut cream
100ml maple syrup
3 tablespoons coconut oil
1 teaspoon vanilla extract
1 tablespoon fresh thyme
 leaves, plus 1 tablespoon
 extra for sprinkling

Preheat the oven to 180°C/160°C Fan/Gas Mark 4. Grease a 20cm round loose-bottomed tart tin with a little oil.

Make the flax 'egg' by mixing the ground flaxseeds and 4 tablespoons of water in a small bowl. Set aside to thicken.

Add the ground almonds, flours, salt and sugar to a large bowl and mix to combine. Add in the oil, almond milk and flax 'egg'. Mix thoroughly with a wooden spoon to form a dough.

Transfer the dough to the tart tin and use your fingers to press into the base and up the sides. Poke a few holes with a fork across the base. Bake for 30 minutes until golden brown, then remove from the oven and allow to cool.

To make the filling, mix the cornflour with 2 tablespoons of water in a small bowl. Stir very well and set aside.

Add the lemon zest and juice, coconut cream, maple syrup, coconut oil, vanilla extract and thyme to a small saucepan and briefly bring to the boil over a medium heat. Turn down the heat to low, and add the cornflour mixture, stirring well. Simmer until thickened. Remove from the heat and set aside to cool briefly.

Pour the filling into the cooled tart base and sprinkle the extra thyme leaves over the top. Transfer to the fridge overnight to set. Serve cold.

This rich and decadent dessert is perfect for a dinner party, especially served with creamy vegan ice cream. I know this because my guests have been treated to this very pie on many occasions and they absolutely love it. Okay, so it's a little indulgent, but it's naturally sweetened with the dates and protein packed from the nuts, so that's acceptable, right? The crust is made from pecans, raw cacao and dates, an amazing combination of sweet and salty. It's incredibly moreish and the salted caramel filling is so good.

Freezer salted caramel pecan pie

Makes 1 x 20cm tart

150g medjool dates, pitted
2 tablespoons peanut butter
    or nut butter of choice
125ml almond milk or plant-
    based milk of choice
2 tablespoons coconut oil
1 teaspoon pink Himalayan salt
150g pecans, to sprinkle
sea salt flakes, to sprinkle

For the pecan crust

100g pecans
40g ground almonds
2 tablespoons flaxseeds
2 tablespoons peanut butter
2 tablespoons raw cacao
8 medjool dates, pitted

To make the crust, add the pecans to a food processor or high-speed blender and blitz. Add in the remaining crust ingredients and blitz again until everything comes together.

Press the crumbly mixture into a 20cm loose-bottomed cake or tart tin with your hands, then put into the freezer while you make the caramel.

Wash out your food processor (or high-speed blender) and add in the dates, peanut butter, milk, coconut oil and salt. Blitz until smooth and creamy – it will be a few minutes before all the dates are thoroughly blended in.

Dollop the caramel onto the pie base and smooth out. Return to the freezer for at least 1 hour to firm up.

Add the pecans to a dry pan and toast over a medium heat for a few minutes, until lightly coloured. Set aside.

Remove the pie from the freezer and decorate the top of the pie with the toasted pecans, starting from the outer edge and creating a concentric circle pattern into the centre. Sprinkle with sea salt flakes.

Store in the freezer. About 30–45 minutes before you want to serve the pie, take it out of the freezer to sit at room temperature.

Malabi –
cardamom, rose *and*
pistachio custard

Cardamom is one of my favourite spices. The scent immediately transports me to India or the Middle East. I love it in savoury dishes but it's even better in desserts. Here it is combined with heavenly pistachio and rose – a dream.

I first ate malabi (Israeli milk pudding) in Israel and immediately fell in love with the combination of flavours. I hope you enjoy my version with its creamy coconut base and that altogether magical combination of pistachio, cardamom and rose.

Serves 4

500ml almond or drinking
   coconut milk
150g coconut cream
2 teaspoons vanilla extract
20 cardamom pods, lightly
   crushed and husks removed
1 teaspoon rose water
4 tablespoons maple syrup
3 tablespoons cornflour
4 tablespoons crushed
   pistachios, to serve

Put all the ingredients except
the cornflour and pistachios in a
saucepan over a medium heat and
stir to combine. Simmer for 2–3
minutes, stirring continuously.

Add the cornflour to a small bowl
along with 2 tablespoons of water
to form a smooth paste, making sure
there are no lumps.

Now add the cornflour mix to
the pan, turn up the heat to
medium–high and stir continuously
to avoid lumps forming. Bring the
mixture briefly to the boil then
reduce the heat to low. Continue
to stir until thickened, then remove
from the heat.

Strain the mixture through
a sieve into a large bowl to remove
the cardamom seeds and any lumps.
Now pour the creamy mix into four
glasses. Allow to cool a little then
pop in the refrigerator overnight
to set.

Serve topped with the
crushed pistachios.

These cookies look a bit like falafels, but that's just camouflage for something pretty special. The fresh ginger and turmeric elevate them above your average spiced biscuit. Fresh turmeric, if you can get it, imbues food with a rich golden hue and has amazing anti-inflammatory properties. But don't worry if you can't find fresh as ground is also amazing and will give the same colour and most of the benefits.

Did I mention the other wholesome ingredients? Ground almonds, mixed seeds, oats, desiccated coconut, coconut oil, lots of spices, banana and a little coconut honey for sweetness. These are one of my favourite things to eat for breakfast on the go.

Spiced turmeric
and
ginger cookies

Makes 30

50g ground almonds
75g gluten-free oats
3 tablespoons sunflower seeds
2 tablespoons ground flaxseeds
2 tablespoons sesame seeds
50g desiccated coconut
a pinch of sea salt flakes
1 teaspoon ground all spice
1 teaspoon ground cinnamon
3 teaspoons ground ginger
1 teaspoon baking powder
4 tablespoons coconut oil
1 ripe banana, peeled
  and mashed
4 tablespoons maple syrup, rice
  malt syrup or coconut honey
2 tablespoons almond butter
1 teaspoon freshly grated
  turmeric or 1½ teaspoons
  ground turmeric
a thumb-sized piece of ginger,
  finely grated

Preheat the oven to 180°C/160°C Fan/Gas Mark 4 and line a baking sheet with baking parchment.

Mix all the dry ingredients in a large bowl. If using ground turmeric, add this now.

Melt the coconut oil in a saucepan over a low heat, then pour into a bowl. Add the banana, maple syrup, almond butter, grated fresh turmeric and ginger to the oil, and mix to combine well. Add the wet ingredients to the dry and mix really well to combine.

Shape the mix into small balls the size of golf balls and pop them onto the lined baking tray spacing them out slightly. Flatten the balls a little using your fingers and bake for 15–20 minutes, until slightly brown. Remove from the oven and transfer to a wire rack to cool.

Coconut and mango are a match made in heaven. It's the taste of tropical holidays and sunshine. These creamy little pots of happiness are super easy to make and perfect for entertaining as you can make ahead and pull out at the appropriate time. Served together with the tahini biscuits ... it's all incredibly good.

Coconut
and
mango panna cotta
with
tahini biscuits

Makes 4

250ml coconut cream
4 tablespoons coconut yoghurt
1 tablespoon coconut oil
1 large ripe mango, peeled
    and destoned
4 tablespoons maple syrup
1 teaspoon vanilla extract
2 tablespoons agar flakes

For the tahini almond biscuits (makes 20)

200g ground almonds
2 tablespoons sesame seeds,
    plus extra to sprinkle
½ teaspoon sea salt flakes
6 tablespoons tahini
4 tablespoons maple syrup
1 teaspoon vanilla extract
1 teaspoon almond extract
1 tablespoon fresh thyme
    leaves

To make the panna cotta, add the coconut cream, yoghurt, oil, mango, maple syrup and vanilla extract to a food processor or high-speed blender. Blitz until very smooth and creamy.

Add the mixture to a small saucepan and add the agar flakes. Let the agar flakes sit in the mixture for 5 minutes to allow them to soften. Bring to the boil without stirring over a medium heat. Lower the heat and simmer, stirring occasionally, for 3–5 minutes or until the agar flakes dissolve. Pour into four 150ml glasses or ramekins. Allow to cool to room temperature, then pop in the fridge to set.

Preheat the oven to 180°C/160°C Fan/Gas Mark 4. Line a baking tray with baking parchment.

Add the ground almonds, sesame seeds and salt to a large bowl and stir well. Stir in the tahini, maple syrup, vanilla and almond extracts and the thyme. Scoop tablespoons of the mixture to get roughly same-sized biscuits, squeezing and rolling each into a ball. Flatten slightly with your fingers and place on the lined tray. Sprinkle with extra sesame seeds.

Bake for 15 minutes, until light golden brown. Remove and allow to cool a little before serving with the chilled panna cotta.

Chocolate, peanut butter *and* chickpea fridge bars

I think this recipe will blow your mind. It seems there's no end to the miraculous things you can make with the humble chickpea. Yes, these amazing chocolate peanut butter fridge brownie bars are made with chickpeas! Not weird, but absolutely delicious. I urge you to try them. And there is no cooking required – simply blend and refrigerate.

I created this recipe with my fellow peanut butter, healthy dessert loving friend Lisa in mind – I hope it meets her approval.

Tip: swap the peanut butter for almond butter and add ½ teaspoon almond essence.

Serves 8–10

400g can of chickpeas, drained
250g medjool dates, pitted
4 tablespoons crunchy
    peanut butter
5 tablespoons raw cacao
3 tablespoons melted
    coconut oil
1 teaspoon vanilla extract
2 tablespoons cacao nibs
2 tablespoons chopped
    hazelnuts, plus extra
    to scatter
40g vegan chocolate
sea salt flakes

Put the chickpeas, dates, peanut
butter, cacao, coconut oil, vanilla
and a generous pinch of sea salt
into a food processor or high-speed
blender. Blitz until you get a smooth
mix. Now add the cacao nibs and
hazelnuts, and pulse once to mix.

Line a 17 x 22cm baking tray with
baking parchment then spoon the
mix into the tray. Smooth out to
the edges.

Gently melt the chocolate in a
small bowl suspended over a small
saucepan of boiling water.

Drizzle the melted chocolate over
the mixture in the tray, then scatter
with some chopped hazelnuts and
sprinkle over a little salt. Refrigerate
for at least 4 hours, or overnight,
to firm up.

Remove from the tray and cut into
squares. The bars are best kept in
the fridge where they will keep for
3–4 days, or store in the freezer
for up to a few weeks.

THE REBEL
PANTRY

Here It Is... Where It All Began Store Cupboard Essentials Quick and Easy Transformative Toast Toppers Brunch Big Vegan Breakfasts Curry for Breakfast Radical Curries and Delectable Dals World Flavours Comfort Food Incredible Pastas and Risottos Small Plates A Soup for All Seasons Salad Bliss Flatbreads and Pizzas Life-changing Pancake Breads Pure Comfort Something Special Tempting Tarts A Little Lighter **Devilish Dips and Sauces 244 Life-changing Dressings 258 Pickle and Preserve Like a Pro 261 Plant-based Milks 268 Nut Butters 270** Index About the Author Acknowledgements Here It Is... Where It All Began Store Cupboard Essentials Quick and Easy Transformative Toast Toppers Brunch Big Vegan Breakfasts Curry for Breakfast Radical Curries and Delectable Dals World Flavours Comfort Food Incredible Pastas and Risottos Small Plates A Soup for All Seasons Salad Bliss Flatbreads and Pizzas Life-changing Pancake Breads Pure Comfort Something Special Tempting Tarts A Little Lighter Devilish Dips and Sauces Life-changing Dressings Pickle and Preserve Like a Pro Plant-based Milks Nut Butters Index About the Author Acknowledgements Here It Is... Where It All Began Store Cupboard Essentials Quick and Easy Transformative Toast Toppers Brunch Big Vegan Breakfasts Curry for Breakfast Radical Curries and Delectable Dals World Flavours Comfort Food Incredible Pastas and Risottos Small Plates A Soup for All Seasons Salad Bliss Flatbreads and Pizzas Life-changing Pancake Breads Pure Comfort Something Special Tempting Tarts A Little Lighter Devilish

Of course I had to include some hummus recipes, and whipping up your own means that you can tailor it to your own tastes (I like to add lots of lemon juice). But what makes hummus even better? Topping it with shakshuka-style veg and scooping it up with spelt flatbread.

Shakshuka hummus *with* spelt flatbread

Serves 4

1 aubergine, cut into 2cm cubes
4 tablespoons olive oil
¼ teaspoon smoked garlic
   powder, optional
2 red or orange peppers,
   deseeded and sliced
   lengthways
6 spring onions, roughly
   chopped
4 garlic cloves, sliced
1 teaspoon cumin seeds
6 tomatoes, roughly chopped
a pinch of dried chilli flakes
2 tablespoons chopped
   olives, optional
1 tablespoon capers, optional
a handful of coriander
sea salt flakes and freshly
   ground black pepper

For the hummus
300g canned chickpeas
2 garlic cloves, peeled
2 tablespoons tahini
3 tablespoons extra virgin olive
   oil, plus extra to drizzle
½ teaspoon cumin seeds
juice of 1–2 lemons
smoked paprika, to sprinkle

Add the chickpeas (reserving 3 tablespoons), garlic, tahini, olive oil, cumin, lemon juice, a pinch of salt and 4 tablespoons of water to a food processor or high-speed blender and blitz until very smooth and creamy (2–3 minutes). Top with extra virgin olive oil and a sprinkle of paprika.

Preheat the oven to 180°C/160°C Fan/Gas Mark 4.

Put the aubergine into a roasting tray and add 2 tablespoons of the olive oil and, if using, the garlic powder. Season with salt and pepper. Toss well to coat. Roast in the oven for approximately 25 minutes, turning occasionally, until soft.

Preheat a griddle pan over a high heat. When hot, add the peppers and char for about 15 minutes, turning frequently until nicely charred on both sides. Remove and set aside, and when they are cool chop quite finely.

Pour the remaining 2 tablespoons of olive oil into a frying pan and add the spring onions, garlic and cumin. Fry over a medium heat for 3–4 minutes, until the spring onions are just starting to colour and get soft. Add the tomatoes and chilli flakes, and season with salt and pepper. Simmer for 15–20 minutes until the tomatoes have broken down. (Note, you may need to keep adding a little water if the mix looks as though it is getting too dry.) Add in the roast peppers and aubergine, stir to combine and simmer for a couple more minutes. If using, stir in the olives and capers and top with fresh coriander.

Make the flatbreads. In a large bowl, combine the flour, baking powder and a pinch of salt. Now add in the yoghurt and 75ml of water, mix thoroughly to combine and then transfer to a floured surface. Knead for a few minutes until you get a rough but springy dough. Pop it back in the bowl for 15 minutes.

For the flatbread

200g spelt flour, plus extra
    for dusting
1 teaspoon baking powder
100g coconut yoghurt or plant-
    based yoghurt of choice

Preheat a griddle pan or frying pan over a medium heat. Divide the dough into four portions, then roll one out on a floured surface to a 20cm round. Pop it on the griddle pan and allow to cook and char a little on one side, then flip to cook the other side. Repeat. Keep the flatbreads warm on a plate covered with a tea towel.

Spread the hummus onto a large platter and top with the shakshuka, reserved chickpeas and a little extra coriander. Scoop up with the flatbreads.

Layering is a bit of a theme with my dishes. I find that different textures and complementary flavours make for a more interesting meal, and dips are no different!

Caramelised onion hummus *and* tapenade *with* thyme crackers

Makes 500g

For the caramelised onion hummus

2 tablespoons olive oil
1 red onion, thinly sliced
400g can of chickpeas (reserve
    3 tablespoons to serve), rinsed
    and drained
1 garlic clove, peeled
3 tablespoons extra virgin olive oil
juice of ½ lemon
sea salt flakes and freshly ground
    black pepper

For the tapenade

100g mixed olives
1 tablespoon capers
2 garlic cloves, peeled and
    roughly chopped
2 tablespoons olive oil
1 teaspoon lemon juice
¼ teaspoon freshly ground
    black pepper
1 tablespoon fresh thyme leaves
20g basil leaves
4 sundried tomatoes

For the thyme crackers

60g buckwheat flour
50g rice flour
50g flaxseeds
3 tablespoons sunflower seeds
25g sesame seeds
3 teaspoons poppy seeds
3 tablespoons fresh thyme leaves
1½ teaspoons sea salt flakes
4 tablespoons olive oil
200ml just-boiled water
a large pinch of dried chilli flakes

Add the olive oil and sliced red onion to a small frying pan and fry very gently over a low heat for 30–40 minutes, until caramelised. Add a big pinch of salt and pepper, and set aside.

Preheat the oven to 150°C/130°C Fan/Gas Mark 2. Line a flat baking sheet with baking parchment.

Make the crackers. Mix the flours, seeds and thyme in a bowl along with ½ teaspoon of the salt. Add the olive oil and just-boiled water, and bring together into a ball of dough. Allow to rest for 5 minutes. Place the dough in the middle of the tray, then place another sheet of baking parchment on top. Use a rolling pin to roll the dough out into a thin layer, about 4mm in thickness. Remove the top piece of parchment paper and sprinkle the dough with the remaining 1 teaspoon of salt flakes and the chilli. Bake for 35 minutes. Remove from the oven and allow to cool, then break into uneven shards.

Next, add the chickpeas, garlic, extra virgin olive oil, lemon juice and 1 teaspoon of salt to a food processor or high-speed blender and blitz until very smooth and creamy (2–3 minutes). Add the caramelised onions and blitz briefly.

Make the tapenade by blitzing all the ingredients together in a food processor or high-speed blender until you get a chunky paste.

Serve the crackers with the tapenade and hummus layered on top.

My classic hummus topped with fresh herbs elevates it to new heights.

Herby pesto hummus

Serves 4

400g can of chickpeas, reserve
  3 tablespoons aquafaba (the
  liquid from the can)
1 garlic clove, peeled
1 tablespoon tahini
1 tablespoon extra virgin olive
  oil, plus extra to drizzle
¼ teaspoon ground cumin
juice of 1–2 lemons
1 teaspoon sea salt flakes
a pinch of smoked paprika
1 tablespoon toasted pine nuts

For the herby pesto

25g basil leaves
25g mint leaves
25g coriander leaves
1 garlic clove, peeled and
  roughly chopped
¼ teaspoon sea salt flakes
2 tablespoons extra virgin
  olive oil
juice of ½ lemon
1 tablespoon toasted pine nuts

Add the chickpeas, garlic, tahini, extra virgin olive oil, cumin, lemon juice, salt and aquafaba to a food processor or high-speed blender and blitz until very smooth and creamy (2–3 minutes). If the hummus seems too stiff, add a splash or two of cold water until you have the desired consistency. Transfer to a bowl and drizzle with extra virgin olive oil and sprinkle with paprika.

Clean out the food processor bowl (or blender) and add all the ingredients for the pesto. Pulse to form a rough paste. Dollop the pesto on top of the hummus and top with the toasted pine nuts.

Here are two incredible pestos that will blow your mind with their intensity of flavour. I always try to have at least one pesto in the fridge as it makes for a speedy meal – pesto pizza, tossed through pasta, or spread on bruschetta and topped with roast tomatoes. Feel free to use any combination of greens, nuts, herbs. My favourites are spinach and pine nut, and basil and brazil nut.

Spinach *and* pine nut pesto

Makes 250g

100g toasted pine nuts
100g spinach
2 tablespoons olive oil
½ teaspoon sea salt flakes
juice of ½ lemon
2 garlic cloves, peeled
75g basil
3 tablespoons nutritional
   yeast flakes

Add all the ingredients to the food processor or high-speed blender and blitz until everything is combined to the texture you prefer. You may need to scrape the sides down a few times.

Basil *and* brazil nut pesto

Serves 2–4

50g basil
100g brazil nuts
1 garlic clove, peeled
4 tablespoons olive oil
½ teaspoon sea salt flakes
a twist of black pepper
3 tablespoons nutritional
   yeast flakes

Add all the ingredients to a food processor or high-speed blender and blitz until everything is combined to the texture you prefer. You may need to scrape the sides down a few times.

Add 2 tablespoons of water to loosen the pesto, or enough water until you get the preferred texture.

Tomato *and* pepper sauce

Makes 4–6 servings

3 red peppers
2 tablespoons olive oil
1 red onion, roughly chopped
3 garlic cloves, sliced
8 large ripe tomatoes, roughly
  chopped or 25 cherry
  tomatoes
6 sundried tomatoes, chopped
½ teaspoon smoked paprika
2 tablespoons tomato purée
a pinch of dried red chilli
  flakes, optional
sea salt flakes and freshly
  ground black pepper

Chargrill the peppers on a griddle pan over a high heat for about 15 minutes, turning frequently until nicely charred all over. Cool a little and roughly chop.

Add the oil and onion to a wide-bottomed frying pan and cook over a low heat for around 10 minutes, or until soft and beginning to brown. Add the garlic and fry for 30 seconds more. Add the fresh and sundried tomatoes, paprika, tomato purée and chopped chargrilled peppers, and season with salt, then cover the pan with the lid. Cook over a low heat for 25 minutes. Add a generous twist of black pepper and, if using, the chilli flakes to the pan and simmer for a further minute.

Homemade harissa paste

Makes 4–6 servings

1 red pepper deseeded and
  chopped in half
2 tablespoons tomato purée
1 tablespoon smoked paprika
¼ teaspoon cayenne pepper
1 teaspoon garlic granules
5 tablespoons extra virgin
  olive oil
1 teaspoon white wine vinegar
½ teaspoon sea salt flakes
juice of 1 lemon

For the spice mix
1 teaspoon cumin seeds
1 teaspoon fennel seeds
2 teaspoons coriander seeds
1 teaspoon dried chilli flakes

Sterilise a small glass Mason jar or similar by washing well in hot soapy water and allowing to dry in a low oven.

Firstly, toast the spice mix ingredients in a dry pan for a couple of minutes, or until fragrant. Now either crush in a pestle and mortar or blitz in a spice grinder.

Chargrill the pepper on a griddle pan over a high heat for around 15 minutes, turning frequently, until it's nice and charred on both sides. Set aside.

Now add all the ingredients to a food processor and blitz to a paste, adding a little water to loosen if needed. Transfer to the clean jar and secure with a lid. Store in the fridge, where it will keep for 1–2 weeks.

Have you tried dukkah? It's a nutty, crunchy, spicy Middle Eastern dip that you sprinkle on your food or dip your bread into. My friend Helen introduced me to dukkah a few years ago and now I make it all the time, although it only lasts about five minutes because my husband and I are addicted.

Traditionally, dukkah is eaten with bread and olive oil. First, the bread is dipped into the olive oil, then into the dukkah. The dukkah sticks on the oily bread and you get a super crunchy, moreish mouthful. However, dukkah is really versatile and can be sprinkled on salads, soups and curries.

Hazelnut *and* thyme dukkah

Makes 175g

100g raw unsalted hazelnuts
1 tablespoon cumin seeds
1 tablespoon coriander seeds
3 tablespoons sesame seeds
2 tablespoons sunflower seeds
1–2 thyme sprigs, leaves picked
1 teaspoon sea salt flakes
½ teaspoon dried chilli flakes

Preheat the oven to 180°C/160°C Fan/Gas Mark 4.

Spread the hazelnuts and seeds over a baking tray lined with parchment paper. Toast for 5 minutes, then remove and allow to cool.

Add the toasted nuts and seeds along with the thyme leaves, salt and chilli flakes to a mini food processor and pulse in one-second bursts – you don't want the dukkah too finely chopped.

variation

By all means the combinations of nuts and herbs can be adapted and tweaked to taste. For a pistachio dukkah just replace the hazelnuts with the same weight of pistachios and swap the thyme for mint instead.

My husband Andy described my beetroot dip as the 'best thing he's ever tasted', but as he says that about most things I cook I'm not sure it counts for much. Having said that, it's a pretty good dip! Earthy beetroots combined with creamy cashews, all topped with sticky maple hazelnuts.

Beetroot dip *with* maple hazelnuts

Makes 500g

3 tablespoons pine nuts
4 beetroots, cooked and peeled
1 garlic clove, peeled
50g cashews, soaked in a bowl
    of water for at least 2 hours
2 tablespoons nutritional
    yeast flakes
2 tablespoons olive oil
sea salt flakes and freshly
    ground black pepper

For the hazelnuts
30g blanched hazelnuts,
    plus extra crushed hazelnuts
    to serve
1 teaspoon maple syrup

Start by toasting the pine nuts in a dry frying pan over a medium heat until lovely and golden.

Put the beetroot into a food processor or high-speed blender. Add the garlic, toasted pine nuts, drained cashews, nutritional yeast flakes, olive oil and 2 tablespoons of water. Blitz until smooth (about 2 minutes), then season with salt and pepper to taste.

For the caramelised hazelnuts, toast the nuts in a dry frying pan, then drizzle in the maple syrup and sprinkle with salt. Set aside. Serve the dip garnished with a handful of crushed hazelnuts.

My latest dip obsession: a creamy, smoky base of roast cauliflower and aubergine with sautéed garlic and almonds topped with blistered roasted cherry tomatoes. I like to serve it with fluffy flatbreads, extra virgin olive oil and dukkah (page 252).

Roast cauliflower, aubergine *and* garlic dip *with* blistered tomatoes

Serves 4–6

1 small cauliflower, broken
   into florets
1 medium aubergine, cut into
   2.5cm slices
3 tablespoons olive oil
1 teaspoon garlic powder
6 garlic cloves, peeled
4 tablespoons flaked almonds
1 tablespoon lemon juice
sea salt flakes and freshly
   ground black pepper

For the blistered
   tomatoes
1 teaspoon smoked paprika
1 teaspoon garlic granules
2 tablespoons olive oil
200g cherry tomatoes,
   chopped in half

To serve
smoked sea salt or regular sea
   salt flakes
extra virgin olive oil

Put the cauliflower florets and aubergine slices in a large roasting tin with 1 tablespoon of the olive oil, 1 teaspoon of salt and the garlic powder. Season with pepper. Roast for 20 minutes, then turn. Continue to roast for a further 20 minutes or until the vegetables are cooked and golden brown. Remove from the oven and allow to cool.

Add the remaining 2 tablespoons oil to a medium saucepan and set over a medium heat. Add the garlic and sauté for a few minutes, until starting to soften and brown. Add in the flaked almonds and cook for a minute or so, until slightly browning. Remove from the heat.

To prepare the blistered tomatoes, add the paprika, garlic granules and 1 tablespoon of the oil to a bowl and combine. Add the cherry tomatoes to the bowl and mix well. Heat the remaining 1 tablespoon of oil in a large frying pan over a medium heat. Place the cherry tomatoes cut-side down into the pan. Fry for 2–3 minutes over a medium-low heat, then turn over and fry for a further minute. Remove from the pan and set aside.

Add the roast veg and garlic, almonds and their oil to a food processor or high-speed blender. Blitz to a smooth paste, then season well with the salt, pepper and lemon juice. Blitz briefly again. Spoon into a bowl, top with the blistered tomatoes, a pinch of smoked salt or sea salt and a drizzle of extra virgin olive oil.

I first created this roast courgette and mint dip to deal with the many courgettes sitting around looking sad in my fridge. If in doubt, I usually roast everything either to make a soup or a dip. On this occasion I combined the roast courgette with fresh mint, tahini and coconut yoghurt for a super creamy dip. For an extra flourish, it's topped with my coconut-mint dressing.

Roast courgette dip *with* coconut mint dressing

Serves 4 as part of a sharing meal

2 medium courgettes, chopped roughly
1 tablespoon rapeseed oil
1 garlic clove, sliced
1 tablespoon tahini
juice of ½ lemon
1 tablespoon coconut yoghurt
a handful of fresh mint leaves
extra virgin olive oil, to drizzle
sea salt flakes and freshly ground black pepper

For the coconut-mint dressing

4 tablespoons coconut yoghurt
1 teaspoon extra virgin olive oil
juice of ½ lemon
½ garlic clove, minced (optional)
a handful of fresh mint leaves, roughly chopped

Preheat the oven to 180°C/160°C Fan/Gas Mark 4.

Add the courgettes to a roasting tray. Toss with the rapeseed oil then roast for 25–30 minutes. Remove and allow to cool.

Add the cooled courgettes, garlic, tahini, lemon juice and yoghurt to a food processor or high-speed blender and blitz to a chunky paste. Add the mint and pulse briefly. Season with about ½ teaspoon of salt and some pepper.

To make the dressing, put all the ingredients into a jar, secure the lid and shake to combine. Season to taste with salt and pepper.

Serve the dip with a drizzle more extra virgin olive oil and a dollop of the coconut-mint dressing.

Garlic aioli

Makes 200ml

3 tablespoons aquafaba
   (liquid drained from a can
   of chickpeas)
1 tablespoon apple cider
   vinegar
½ teaspoon Dijon mustard
½ teaspoon sea salt flakes
2 garlic cloves, peeled
125ml vegetable oil or
   rapeseed oil
1 teaspoon lemon juice

Add the aquafaba, vinegar, mustard, salt and garlic to
a mini food processor and blitz to combine.

Keeping the food processor running constantly, very
slowly drizzle in the oil.

The aioli will become think and creamy; at this point stir
in the lemon juice. Transfer to a jar with a lid and keeps
in the fridge for 1–2 days.

.

I say that these dressings are life changing because a good dressing
really can transform your meals in minutes. They add so much flavour,
and fats, acids and salt. Here are some of my favourites – I can't live
without them.

Caper dressing

Makes 200ml

a small handful of mint and
   coriander, chopped
juice of ½ lemon
2 cocktail gherkins,
   finely chopped
2 tablespoons capers
6 tablespoons extra virgin
   olive oil
1 garlic clove, finely sliced
sea salt flakes and freshly
   ground black pepper

Add all the ingredients to a jar, replace the lid and shake
to combine. Keep for 2–3 days in the fridge.

Herby tahini dressing

Makes 130ml

1 clove of garlic
1 tablespoon tahini
juice of ½ lemon
a small handful of mint
a small handful of coriander
sea salt flakes and freshly
    ground black pepper

Add the ingredients to a mini food processor with
3 tablespoons of water and blitz.

If you don't have a mini food processor, just crush the
garlic to a paste in a pestle and mortar and then add all
the ingredients to a jar and shake to combine.

It will keep for 2–3 days in the fridge.

Satay dressing

Makes 140ml

1 tablespoon tamari
1 teaspoon sriracha sauce
2 tablespoons toasted
    sesame oil
3 tablespoons coconut milk
1 teaspoon maple syrup
¼ teaspoon brown rice miso
2 tablespoons chunky
    peanut butter
½ teaspoon garlic granules
½ teaspoon dried chilli flakes

Add all the ingredients to a jar, replace the lid and shake
to combine.

This keeps for 2–3 days in the fridge.

Ultimate Dijon dressing

Makes 100ml

2 tablespoons extra virgin
  olive oil
4 tablespoons apple
  cider vinegar
2 teaspoons Dijon mustard
2 teaspoons maple syrup
sea salt flakes and freshly
  ground black pepper

Add all the ingredients to a jar, replace the lid and shake to combine.

This keeps for 2–3 days in the fridge.

Lime *and* coriander dressing

Makes 140ml

grated zest and juice of 1 lime
2 tablespoons capers
2 tablespoons olive oil
2 garlic cloves, sliced
2 tablespoons white
  wine vinegar
1 teaspoon wholegrain mustard
2 tablespoons finely chopped
  coriander
½ teaspoon maple syrup
dried chilli flakes, optional
sea salt flakes and freshly
  ground black pepper

Add all the ingredients to a jar, replace the lid and shake to combine.

This dressing will keep for 2–3 days in the fridge.

Sauerkraut is deceptively easy to make. Once you've done it a few times, you can start to experiment with flavour combinations, adding your favourite blend of herbs and spices. I have a portion of sauerkraut or kimchi every day. I love it.

Cabbage *and* carrot sauerkraut

Makes 1 x 2-litre jar

500g white cabbage
500g red cabbage,
  finely chopped
200g carrots, finely grated
2 teaspoons sea salt flakes
1 teaspoon cumin seeds
1 teaspoon grated ginger

Peel away an outer leaf from the white cabbage and set aside. Finely chop the cabbage and transfer it, along with the red cabbage and carrots, to a large bowl. Add the salt and mix well. Sprinkle the cumin seeds and ginger over the veg. Use your hands to massage the mix for a few minutes to release the liquid from the veg, and to allow the cabbage to soften a little.

In a large sterilised jar (such as a 2-litre Kilner jar or use 2 x 1-litre jars), add the mixture along with any liquid that has seeped out of the veg. Press down to ensure the mixture is about 2cm clear from the top of the jar.

Cover the surface of the mix with the reserved large leaf of cabbage and press down so that the mixture is submerged in liquid. Add more water to top up if necessary. In a (sterilised) jar small enough to fit inside the larger jar, put dried beans in and close its lid. Place the bean-filled jar on top of the cabbage leaf and, to hold it in place, close the lid of the main jar.

Leave for 3 days to ferment, checking regularly that the mixture is submerged in the liquid and tasting until you're happy. Transfer to the fridge and store for up to 5 months.

Kimchi, I absolutely love it. In fact, I find most fermented foods delicious, which is lucky as they're super healthy. I try to include them in my diet most days to encourage healthy gut-bacteria.

I first discovered kimchi many years ago at a Korean restaurant and became hooked. To be honest, I very often buy an incredible local vegan kimchi but if you want to eat it as much as I do it's good to make your own. I've also included a cauliflower version – I think you'll love it.

Kick-ass kimchi

Makes 1 x 1-litre jar

½ small cabbage (preferably napa if you can get it)
1 teaspoon sea salt flakes
1 small carrot, grated
¼ red pepper, sliced into very thin strips (or julienned)

For the kimchi paste

½ red pepper, deseeded and chopped
1 tablespoon finely minced ginger
3 garlic cloves, minced
1 spring onion, sliced
2 teaspoons gochugaru (Korean chilli powder) or 1–2 teaspoons dried chilli flakes mixed with 1 teaspoon smoked paprika
2 teaspoons maple syrup or sweetener of choice
1 teaspoon sea salt flakes
1 teaspoon miso paste, optional

Sterilise a 1-litre glass Mason jar or similar by washing well in hot soapy water and allowing to dry in a low oven.

Rinse the cabbage and then slice into small bite-sized pieces. Add to a large bowl and use clean hands to massage the salt into the cabbage, ensuring all the surfaces are coated in salt, about 5 minutes. Leave to sit for 30 minutes for the cabbage to soften.

Meanwhile, add all the ingredients for the paste to a food processor. Blitz to form a paste.

Add the carrot and pepper to the bowl with the cabbage and massage the paste into the vegetables, using clean hands. Try to thoroughly coat the cabbage in the paste.

Pack the mixture into the jar, firmly pressing down but allowing at least 4cm clear from the top of the jar. Pour over any liquid collected in the bowl, making sure the cabbage is completely submerged in liquid. Top up with water if necessary.

Secure the jar lid and store away from sunlight for 2–3 days. Remove the lid once a day to allow gases to be released and check the cabbage is covered in liquid (topping up with a little water if needed).

Taste the kimchi after a few days; it should be ready to transfer to the fridge where it will keep for at least 3 months.

Cauliflower kimchi

Makes 1 x 1-litre jar

500g cauliflower head
2 teaspoons sea salt flakes
8 garlic cloves, peeled
a thumb-sized piece of ginger,
   peeled and grated
1 red onion, chopped
1 apple, peeled, cored
and grated
2 teaspoons maple syrup or
   sweetener of choice
3 tablespoons gochugaru
   (Korean chilli powder)
   or 2 teaspoons dried chilli
   flakes plus 1 teaspoon
   smoked paprika
2 tablespoons crumbled nori

Sterilise a 1-litre glass Mason jar or similar by washing well in hot soapy water and allowing to dry in a low oven.

Cut the cauliflower into small florets and chop the leaves and stalks into slices. Add to a large bowl with the salt. Use clean hands to massage the salt into the cauliflower for a few minutes, then put in a colander set over a bowl and leave to sit for 30 minutes to drain. Place the drained cauliflower in a large bowl and reserve the liquid.

To make the paste, add the garlic, ginger, onion, apple, maple syrup and gochugaru to a food processor and blitz with 150ml of water. Transfer the paste to the bowl with the cauliflower and massage in well. Stir in the crumbled nori.

Pack the mixture into the jar and pour over any liquid from the mixing bowl plus the liquid reserved from draining the cauliflower in the first step. Firmly press down on the mixture making sure it is completely submerged in liquid. You can top up with water if needed. (Be careful not to over fill and ensure to allow about 4cm clear from the top of the jar.)

Secure the jar lid and store away from sunlight for 2–3 days. Remove the lid once a day to allow the gases to be released and to check the cauliflower is covered in liquid (you can add a little more water if needed). After a few days the kimchi should be ready to transfer to the fridge where it will keep for at least 3 months.

There are a few things you have in your fridge that can transform meals in minutes, and this is one of the best.

My favourite ways to use this tomato confit include: warming it with a little oil and loading it onto toasted sourdough; stirring it into pesto, tomato pasta or stews; or swirling it into farinata (page 195) or omelettes. All are equally amazing.

Make this in the summer when cherry tomatoes are plentiful and bursting with flavour.

Cherry tomato confit

Makes 1 x 500ml jar

500g assorted cherry tomatoes
– slice half of them in half
6 garlic cloves
2 tablespoons extra virgin olive oil, plus extra to cover
a pinch of coarse sea salt flakes
½ teaspoon freshly ground black pepper
¼ teaspoon dried chilli flakes
2–3 thyme sprigs

Preheat the oven to 140°C/120°C Fan/Gas Mark 1.

Spread the tomatoes, cut side up, and garlic cloves in a large casserole dish or roasting tray. They should fill the dish/tray in a single layer. Drizzle with the extra virgin olive oil and sprinkle with the salt, pepper, chilli and thyme sprigs. Toss gently to coat. Roast for 2 hours or until the tomatoes are shrivelled and some have burst. Remove and allow to cool to room temperature.

Sterilise a glass jar by washing well in hot soapy water and allow to dry in a low oven.

Spoon the cooled tomatoes and garlic into the jars, discard the thyme sprigs, then pour the remaining oil and tomato juices from the dish into the jars to cover. Pour in a little more oil to ensure the tomatoes and garlic are submerged. Seal and store in the fridge for up to 4 weeks.

Pickles are one of my store cupboard essentials. They have the ability to transform, add depth of flavour and brighten any meal. It's not surprising that pickles are served alongside meals in Japanese, Indian and many other cuisines. It's time to embrace the pickle.

Pickles – piccalilli

Makes 1 x 1-litre jar

350ml white wine vinegar
1 tablespoon coriander seeds
1 tablespoon cumin seeds
a pinch of sea salt flakes
½ large cauliflower, broken into small florets
¼ head broccoli, broken into small florets
½ red onion, roughly chopped
75g shallots, sliced
1 small bulb fennel, sliced
1 tablespoon mustard powder
1 tablespoon plain flour
1 tablespoon ground turmeric
1 teaspoon ground ginger
50ml apple cider vinegar
½ small red chilli, sliced
50g green beans, trimmed and finely sliced
1 small apple, cored and grated
2 garlic cloves, sliced
75g sugar

Sterilise a 1-litre glass Mason jar or similar by washing well in hot soapy water and allowing to dry in a low oven.

Add the vinegar, coriander and cumin seeds and salt to a large pan and bring to a boil. Now add the cauliflower, broccoli, onion, shallots and fennel. Reduce the heat to low and simmer for 5 minutes.

In a small bowl, add the mustard powder, flour, turmeric and ginger, and gradually whisk in the apple cider vinegar until smooth. Set aside.

Add the chilli, green beans, apple, garlic and sugar to the pan and stir over the heat for 2–3 minutes, or until the sugar has dissolved. Drain the vegetables over a large bowl to collect the vinegar.

Now add the mustard mixture and the vinegar back into the pan and bring to the boil over a medium-high heat. Reduce the heat to medium–low and simmer for 10 minutes, or until thick enough to coat the back of a spoon, adding more salt if needed.

Return the drained vegetables to the pan and add more sugar and water to taste if necessary and then take off the heat.

Spoon into the warm sterilised jar, seal and allow to cool. Store for 3 months in a cool, dark place before eating. Once opened, keep refrigerated for up to 4 weeks.

Crushed cucumber

Serves 4–6 as a side

2 cucumbers
a pinch of sea salt flakes
1 teaspoon brown rice vinegar
1 teaspoon tamari
1 tablespoon toasted
  sesame oil
1 tablespoon dried chilli flakes
1 tablespoon mirin
1 garlic clove, grated
a small handful (about 15g)
  of coriander, chopped
2 tablespoons toasted
  sesame seeds

Firstly, trim the cucumbers and peel the skins. Cut the cucumbers in half through the middle, then roughly chop into large pieces. Now smash the cucumber with a heavy knife or pestle. Transfer to a colander set over a large bowl. Sprinkle with salt, mix well and set aside for the cucumber to drain for about 10 minutes.

Drain away the excess liquid and return the cucumber to the bowl. Stir in the remaining ingredients to combine and it's ready to eat.

Cucumber *and* dill pickle

Makes 1 x 750ml jar

1 cucumber, sliced into rounds
125ml apple cider vinegar
250ml filtered water
3 tablespoons agave or
  maple syrup
4 tablespoons sea salt flakes
1 tablespoon pink or black
  peppercorns
1 tablespoon mustard seeds
1 tablespoon coriander seeds
1 teaspoon dried chilli flakes
3 tablespoons chopped dill

Sterilise a jar by washing thoroughly in hot soapy water and allowing to dry in a cool oven.

Pop all the ingredients into the sterilised jar. Make sure everything is submerged in the liquid ingredients, or add more water to top up if necessary. Screw on the lid.

Leave at room temperature for 7 days to ferment. Store in the fridge where it will keep for 2 weeks.

Okay, so there are many amazing plant-based milk options out there now (which is fantastic), but if you want to know exactly what's going into your milk – and have the option to play around with flavours – it's a good idea to make your own. It's so easy. Feel free to use a nut milk bag (available from organic stores or online) if you want super smooth milk. Use up any strained nut pulp in flatbread dough or add it to energy bars or cake batter.

Almond *or* hazelnut milk

Makes 1 litre

100g almonds or hazelnuts, soaked in water for 4 hours
2–3 pitted dates or 1 teaspoon maple syrup, optional
1 teaspoon vanilla extract
a pinch of sea salt flakes
1 litre filtered water
1 tablespoon melted coconut oil, optional

Drain and rinse the soaked nuts. Add the nuts, dates, vanilla, sea salt, water and, if using, the oil, to a high-speed blender or nut milk maker. Blitz well for 30 seconds to 1 minute until the milk is smooth and creamy.

You can strain the milk through a nut milk bag or muslin. If you don't mind the milk a bit thicker with pulpy bits leave it as is. Pour into a glass bottle for storage in the fridge where it will keep for up to 4 days.

chocolate milk variation

Add 2 tablespoons of raw cacao powder and 1 tablespoon of maca to the blender along with the other ingredients.

Creamy cashew milk

Makes 1 litre

100g cashews, soaked in water for at least 4 hours
a pinch of sea salt flakes
1 litre filtered water
1 tablespoon melted coconut oil, optional
2–3 pitted dates, optional
1 teaspoon vanilla extract, optional

Drain and rinse the soaked nuts. Add the nuts, sea salt and water to a high-speed blender or nut milk maker. Add the oil, dates and, if using, the vanilla. Blitz well for 30 seconds to 1 minute until the milk is smooth and creamy.

You can strain the milk through a nut milk bag or muslin. If you don't mind the milk a bit thicker with pulpy bits leave it as is. Pour into glass bottles for storage in the fridge where it will keep for up to 4 days.

Sunflower *or* pumpkin seed milk

Makes 1 litre

100g sunflower seeds, soaked
    in water overnight
2 pitted dates, optional
1 teaspoon vanilla extract
½ teaspoon sea salt flakes
½ tablespoon coconut oil
1 litre filtered water

Drain the seeds and add to a high-speed blender or
nut milk maker along with the dates, vanilla, sea salt,
coconut oil and water. Blitz well for 30 seconds to
1 minute until the milk is smooth and creamy.

You can strain the milk through a nut milk bag or muslin.
If you don't mind the milk a bit thicker with pulpy bits
leave it as is. Pour into a glass bottle for storage in the
fridge where it will keep for up to 4 days.

Oat milk

Makes 1 litre

100g rolled oats, soaked in
    water for 20 minutes
1 litre filtered water
2 medjool dates, pitted,
    optional
1 teaspoon vanilla
    extract, optional
a small pinch of sea salt
    flakes, optional

Drain the oats and rinse at least three times in
fresh water.

Add the rinsed oats and 1 litre of filtered water and,
if using, the dates, vanilla and sea salt to a high-speed
blender. Blitz well for 30 seconds to 1 minute until the
milk is smooth and creamy, adding more water if you
prefer a thinner milk.

You can strain the milk through a nut milk bag or muslin.
If you don't mind the milk a bit thicker with pulpy bits
leave it as is. Pour into a glass bottle for storage in the
fridge where it will keep for up to 4 days.

Nut butters, oh how I love you! Spread them on your toast, stir them into oats, dollop them into curries. Not to mention they're the key component to so many desserts. A nut butter is easy to make from scratch. You know exactly what's in them and you have the freedom to tweak the flavours to your desire. Try varying the nuts or playing around with extras, such as adding vanilla or cinnamon.

Crunchy peanut butter

Makes 500g

400g raw peanuts
1 tablespoon groundnut oil
1–2 tablespoons maple syrup,
    to taste
½ teaspoon sea salt flakes, or
    to taste

Preheat the oven to 180°C/160°C Fan/Gas Mark 4.

Add the peanuts to a large baking tray along with the groundnut oil. Roast for 10 minutes, until evenly browned. Remove and allow to cool.

Transfer the nuts to a food processor or high-speed blender and blitz to coarse crumbs (reserve about a quarter of the nuts to make crunchy peanut butter). Continue to blitz until you have a smooth, creamy texture. You may need to scrape down the sides. Add the maple syrup and salt and blitz for a few seconds more. Remove and stir through the reserved nuts if using. Spoon into a jar. It will keep in the fridge for 6–8 weeks.

Almond butter

Makes 350g

300g raw blanched almonds
3 tablespoons maple syrup
1 tablespoon groundnut or
    sunflower oil
½ teaspoon sea salt flakes

Preheat the oven to 140°C/120°C Fan/Gas Mark 1.

Pop the almonds on a baking tray with the maple syrup, oil and salt. Toss to combine.

Roast in the oven for 10–15 minutes, or until a shade darker. Remove and allow to cool.

Transfer the nuts to a food processor or high-speed blender and blitz for a few minutes to break up, scraping down the sides as you go. Blitz for 10 minutes, until lovely and creamy in texture: the longer you blend the smoother the texture.

Transfer to an airtight jar and store in the fridge where it will keep for 6–8 weeks.

Cacao almond spread

Makes 600g

300g almonds
4 tablespoons coconut oil
4 tablespoons raw
  cacao powder
4–6 tablespoons maple syrup
a pinch of sea salt flakes

Preheat the oven to 140°C/120°C Fan/Gas Mark 1.

Pop the almonds on a baking tray and toast in the oven for about 10 minutes, until a shade darker. Remove and allow to cool.

Transfer the nuts to a food processor or high-speed blender and blitz until you have a fine powder (reserve ¼ cup of whole almonds to add in later if you like your nut butter chunky).

Gently melt the coconut oil in a saucepan. Pour into the food processor. Add the cacao, maple syrup and salt and blitz again to get a paste. Next, gradually add 150ml of water until you get the consistency you want. If you have reserved some almonds, crush them a little (with a pestle and mortar) and stir into the mixture. Spoon into a sterilised jar and store in the fridge for up to 6 weeks.

Tahini

Makes 200ml

150g sesame seeds
a pinch of sea salt flakes
4 tablespoons sesame oil
  (not toasted)

Using a powerful high-speed blender or food processor, add the sesame seeds and salt. Blitz until you have a smooth, creamy texture. Gradually add in the oil, scraping down the sides as you go. Store in the fridge where it will keep for up to 3 weeks.

the END

Here It Is... Where It All Began Store Cupboard Essentials Quick and Easy Transformative Toast Toppers Brunch Big Vegan Breakfasts Curry for Breakfast Radical Curries and Delectable Dals World Flavours Comfort Food Incredible Pastas and Risottos Small Plates A Soup for All Seasons Salad Bliss Flatbreads and Pizzas Life-changing Pancake Breads Pure Comfort Something Special Tempting Tarts A Little Lighter Devilish Dips and Sauces Life-changing Dressings Pickle and Preserve Like a Pro Plant-based Milks Nut Butters **Index 274** **About the Author 280** **Acknowledgements 283** Here It Is... Where It All Began Store Cupboard Essentials Quick and Easy Transformative Toast Toppers Brunch Big Vegan Breakfasts Curry for Breakfast Radical Curries and Delectable Dals World Flavours Comfort Food Incredible Pastas and Risottos Small Plates A Soup for All Seasons Salad Bliss Flatbreads and Pizzas Life-changing Pancake Breads Pure Comfort Something Special Tempting Tarts A Little Lighter Devilish Dips and Sauces Life-changing Dressings Pickle and Preserve Like a Pro Plant-based Milks Nut Butters Index About the Author Acknowledgements Here It Is... Where It All Began Store Cupboard Essentials Quick and Easy Transformative Toast Toppers Brunch Big Vegan Breakfasts Curry for Breakfast Radical Curries and Delectable Dals World Flavours Comfort Food Incredible Pastas and Risottos Small Plates A Soup for All Seasons Salad Bliss Flatbreads and Pizzas Life-changing Pancake Breads Pure Comfort Something Special Tempting Tarts A Little Lighter Devilish Dips and Sauces Life-

Index

A

aioli 143, 173, 258
almond milk 268
   date, oat and cardamom
      pudding 64
almonds
   butter 270
   cacao spread 271
   cherry Bakewell chia parfaits 22
   cherry tart with whipped
      cream 226
   chocolate and chestnut brownie
      cake 220
aubergine
   and cauliflower and garlic dip 256
   with lentils and roast
      cauliflower 126
   miso and maple-glazed 95
   moussaka 100
   and pesto bake 110
   roast Sabih 96
   roast with courgettes 143
   spiced pide 189
Autumn – creamy roast cauliflower,
   butter bean and thyme soup 166
avocados
   chocolate truffles 219
   and rainbow slaw 156
   and roast tomato soup 165
   on toast with butter bean and
      thyme hummus 35

B

Baked mushrooms with cashew
   cheese in a rich tomato and
   pepper sauce 108

Baked mushrooms with spinach and
   hazelnut pesto 53
Baked squashes with a nutty
   mushroom filling 120
Baked tahini coconut cheesecake
   with ginger pecan crust and warm
   berries 214
bananas
   peanut butter and choc frappé
      pots 31
   and peanut butter crumble 206
   and peanut butter toastie 38
   sticky sesame with coconut
      porridge 25
basil-cashew cream 159; see also
   pestos
beans
   white bean, coconut and pepper
      stew 116
   see also butter beans; green
      beans; haricot beans
beetroot
   dip with hazelnuts 253
   risotto with hazelnuts and cashew
      'parmesan' 136
Best chocolate ganache tart 224
Big breakfast shakshuka 55
biscuits
   tahini 239
   thyme crackers 246
   turmeric and ginger cookies 236
blackberries
   compote 200
   warm with tahini oats 26
brazil nuts and basil pesto 250
bread
   cheat's injera 88
   farinata with kale pesto 195
   flatbread 96
   panzanella salad 183
   rye roti 63
   salted date and pecan buns 210
   spelt flatbread 244

   spelt soda 200
   see also toast
Breakfast curry with quick rye
   roti 63
broccoli roast with satay
   dressing 154
butter beans
   and cauliflower soup 166
   and roast veg salad 179
   and thyme hummus 35
butternut squash
   baked with mushroom filling 120
   hasselback three ways 150
   risotto with marinara sauce 128

C

cabbage
   and carrot sauerkraut 261
   rainbow slaw with miso
      dressing 156
   salad 70
cacao
   almond spread 271
   peanut butter and choc frappé
      pots 31
cakes
   chocolate, almond and chestnut
      brownie 220
   ginger and chestnut 209
capers dressing 258
Caramelised banana and peanut
   butter crumble with cardamom
   custard 206
Caramelised onion and chickpea
   frittata with roast balsamic
   tomatoes 42
Caramelised onion hummus
   and tapenade with thyme
   crackers 246

cardamom
custard 206
date and oat milk pudding 64
malabi custard 234

carrots
and cabbage sauerkraut 261
warm roast salad 178

cashew cheese
with baked mushrooms 108
on toast 36

cashew nuts
basil sauce 159
milk 268
'parmesan' 136, 144
ricotta 134

cauliflower
and aubergine and garlic dip 256
carbonara with crispy kale 133
curry 76
harissa roast with lentils and
    aubergine 126
kimchi 263
Middle Eastern platter 184
soup with butter bean and
    thyme 166
steaks with polenta and lentil
    ragu 121
and sweet potato and peanut
    stew 115
Chana masala with coconut
    chutney 81
cheese see cashew cheese
'Cheesy' mushrooms and spinach
    on toast 47

cherries
almond tart with whipped
    cream 226
Bakewell chia parfaits 22
chocolate ganache espresso
    pots 215
Cherry tomato confit 264

chestnuts
chocolate and almond brownie
    cake 220
and ginger cake 209
chia cherry Bakewell parfaits 22
chickpeas
chana masala 81
chana masala pizza 190

chocolate and peanut butter
    fridge bars 240
and lentil soup 170
moussaka 100
and mushroom korma 85
and onion frittata 42
roast veg tray bake 159
see also hummus

chocolate
almond and chestnut brownie
    cake 220
avocado truffles 219
cherry ganache espresso
    pots 215
easy tiramisu pots 223
ganache tart 224
milk 268
peanut butter and chickpea fridge
    bars 240
see also cacao

chutney
coconut 58, 76, 81
sweet onion 58
tomato 86

coconut 16
chana masala pizza with mint
    yoghurt 190
chutney 58, 76, 81
dal with cabbage salad and
    toasted seeds 70
easy tiramisu pots 223
and mango lassi 28
and mango panna cotta 239

coconut milk
date, oat and cardamom
    pudding 64
malabi custard 234
sticky rice 95

coconut yoghurt
cherry Bakewell chia parfaits 22
mint 190
mint dip 189
mint dressing 257
spiced porridge with sesame
    banana 25
tahini cheesecake 214
tzatziki 147
and white bean and pepper
    stew 116

coffee
cherry chocolate ganache
    espresso pots 215
easy tiramisu pots 223
condiments 17
coriander
dressing 170
and lime dressing 260
courgettes
dip 257
and roast aubergine, aioli and
    dukkah 143
Creamy mushroom and chickpea
    korma 85
Creamy spiced coconut porridge
    with sticky sesame banana 25
crepes
rava dosa 86
spiced with coconut and sweet
    onion chutneys 58
spinach with caponata and basil
    pesto 48
strawberry and peanut butter 43
Crushed potatoes with rocket pesto
    and cashew 'parmesan' 144
cucumber
crushed 267
and dill pickle 267
and tomato salad 96
curries
breakfast with rye roti 63
cauliflower 76
chana masala 81
gobi matar keema 86
mushroom and chickpea
    korma 85
peanut, sweet potato and veg 74
tomato 82
see also dal

D

dal 19
coconut 70
tarka 76

dates
    and caramel pecan buns 210
    and oat and cardamom milk
        pudding 64
dill
    and cucumber pickle 267
    pesto 165
dips
    beetroot with hazelnuts 253
    cauliflower, aubergine and
        garlic 256
    coconut mint 189
    courgette 257
    mint 190
    see also aioli; dukkahs
dressings
    caper 258
    coconut mint 257
    coriander 170
    Dijon 260
    herby tahini 259
    lime and coriander 260
    miso 156
    satay 154, 259
    tahini 96, 100, 179
    tahini coriander 56
    zaatar 179
drinks coconut and mango lassi 28
dukkahs 143
    hazelnut 179
    hazelnut and thyme 252
    sunflower seed 144
dumplings
    gyozas two ways 102
    hoisin mushroom momos 107

E

Easy tiramisu pots 223
egg replacers 16
Ethiopian platter with cheat's
    injera 88

F

Farinata with kale pesto 195
Flourless chocolate, almond and
    chestnut brownie cake 220
flours 18
Freezer salted caramel pecan
    pie 233
fruit
    lemon and thyme tart 230
    pomegranate 143
    strawberry and peanut butter
        crepes 43
    see also bananas; blackberries;
        cherries; dates; mango

G

Gado Gado with crispy tofu 174
garlic
    aioli 143, 173, 258
    cauliflower and aubergine
        dip 256
ginger
    and chestnut cake 209
    and turmeric cookies 236
Gobi matar keema with tomato
    chutney and rava dosa 86
green beans thoran 76
greens
    sautéed 88
    with tofu and fried rice 92
Gyozas two ways 102

H

haricot beans Masala beans on
    toast 32
Hasselback squash three ways 150
hazelnuts
    beetroot dip 253

caramelised with beetroot
    risotto 136
    dukkah 179
    milk 268
    and spinach pesto 53
    and thyme dukkah 252
Heirloom tomato tart with a walnut
    base 151
herbs 15
    herby rice 100
    tahini dressing 259
    zhoug 96
    see also basil; coriander; dill; mint;
        pestos; thyme
Hoisin mushroom momos 107
Homemade harissa paste 251
hummus 96
    butter bean and thyme 35
    caramelised onion 246
    herby pesto 247
    shakshuka with spelt
        flatbread 244
    turmeric 82

K

kale
    with cauliflower carbonara 133
    mushroom and ricotta lasagne
        134
    pesto 110, 195
    and tomatoes with oatcakes 199
kimchi 262
    cauliflower 263
    cheese on toast 36
    fried rice with greens and tofu 92
    tofu gyoza 102

L

Layered aubergine and pesto
    bake 110
lemon and thyme tart 230

lentils
  and chickpea soup 170
  Ethiopian platter 88
  with harissa cauliflower and
    aubergine 126
  ragu 121
  and roast carrot salad 178
  and veg bake 125
  see also dal
Liberating lemon curd and thyme
  tart 230
lime and coriander dressing 260
Loaded Kim-cheese on toast 36
Loaded Middle Eastern cauliflower
  platter 184

M

Malabi – cardamom, rose and
  pistachio custard 234
mango
  and coconut lassi 28
  and coconut panna cotta 239
maple syrup glazed aubergine 95
Masala beans on toast 32
milks 17; *see also* almond milk;
  coconut milk
mint
  coconut dip 189
  coconut dressing 257
  and pea soup 162
  yoghurt 190
miso
  dressing 156
  and maple-glazed aubergine with
    sticky coconut rice 95
Moussaka 100
Multi-coloured tomato salad
  with sunflower seed crumble
  and aioli 173
mushrooms
  and baked squashes 120
  baked with cashew cheese,
    tomato and pepper sauce 108
  baked with spinach and hazelnut
    pesto 53

  and chickpea korma 85
  hoisin momos 107
  kale and ricotta lasagne 134
  spicy gyoza 102
  and spinach on toast 47
mustard Dijon dressing 260

N

natural sweeteners 16–17
nuts 15
  basil and brazil nut pesto 250
  spinach and pine nut pesto 250
  see also almonds; cashew nuts;
    chestnuts; hazelnuts; peanuts;
    pecan nuts; walnuts
Nutty tahini overnight oats with
  warm blackberries 26

O

oats
  cherry Bakewell chia parfaits 22
  date and cardamom milk
    pudding 64
  milk 269
  spiced coconut porridge with
    sesame banana 25
  tahini overnight with
    blackberries 26
oils 16
olives tapenade 246
onions
  caramelised hummus 246
  and chickpea frittata 42
  chutney 58
Open lasagne with sautéed
  mushrooms, cashew ricotta, kale
  and truffle oil 134
Organic Trade Board 166

P

pancakes
  Staffordshire oatcakes with
    tomatoes and kale 199
  see also crepes
pasta
  cauliflower carbonara with crispy
    kale 133
  lasagne with mushrooms, ricotta,
    kale and truffle oil 134
peanut butter
  and banana crumble 206
  and banana toastie 38
  and choc frappé pots 31
  chocolate and chickpea fridge
    bars 240
  crunchy 270
  frosting 209
  satay dressing 154, 259
  and strawberry crepes 43
peanuts
  sauce 174
  and sweet potato and cauliflower
    stew 115
  and sweet potato and veg
    curry 74
  see also peanut butter
peas
  and mint soup 162
  and new potato salad 147
pecan nuts
  ginger crust cheesecake 214
  salted caramel pie 233
  and salted date buns 210
peppers
  harissa paste 251
  and tomato sauce 251
  and tomato sauce with baked
    mushrooms 108
  and white bean and coconut
    stew 116
pestos
  basil 48
  basil and brazil nut 250
  dill 165
  hummus 247

and roast tomato flatbread
pizza 194
spinach and pine nut 250
Piccalilli 266
pickles
crushed cucumber 267
cucumber and dill 267
piccalilli 266
pine nuts spinach pesto 250
pizza
coconut chana masala 190
pesto and roast tomato 194
spiced aubergine pide 189
polenta with cauliflower steaks 121
pomegranate 143
potatoes
crushed with rocket pesto and
cashew 'parmesan' 144
roast new potato salad 147
spiced with spinach 67
sticky tamarind 160
see also sweet potato
pulses 19; *see also* beans;
chickpeas; lentils
pumpkin seeds milk 269

R

Rainbow slaw with miso dressing,
avocado and toasted seeds 156
rice 19
arancini balls 128
beetroot risotto with
hazelnuts 136
herby 100
kimchi fried with greens and
tofu 92
roast squash risotto 128
sticky coconut 95
Roast aubergine and courgettes
with garlic aioli, pomegranate and
dukkah 143
Roast aubergine Sabih 96
Roast broccoli with satay
dressing 154
Roast cauliflower, aubergine and

garlic dip with blistered
tomatoes 256
Roast cauliflower carbonara with
crispy kale 133
Roast courgette dip with coconut
mint dressing 257
Roast new potato salad with tzatziki
and peas 147
Roast squash risotto or arancini balls
with the best marinara sauce 128
Roast veg salad with butter beans
and hazelnut dukkah 179
rocket pesto 144

S

salads
cabbage 70
cucumber and tomato 96
Gado Gado 174
panzanella 183
roast new potato with tzatziki and
peas 147
roast veg with butter beans 179
slaw with miso dressing 156
tomato with sunflower seed
crumble 173
warm roast carrot 178
Salted date and salted caramel
pecan buns 210
Satay dressing 259
seasoning 18
seeds 15
cherry Bakewell chia parfaits 22
milk 269
see also sunflower seeds
Shakshuka hummus with spelt
flatbread 244
Smoky lentils and harissa roast
cauliflower with aubergine 126
soups
pea and mint 162
roast cauliflower, butter bean and
thyme 166
roast tomato with dill pesto 165
spiced lentil and chickpea 170

Spelt soda bread with nut butter and
warm blackberries 200
Spiced aubergine pide 189
Spiced crepes with coconut chutney
and sweet onion chutney 58
Spiced potatoes and spinach 67
Spiced turmeric and ginger
cookies 236
spices 14
zhoug 96
see also cardamom
spinach
crepes with caponata and basil
pesto 48
and hazelnut pesto 53
and mushrooms on toast 47
and pine nut pesto 250
with spiced potatoes 67
Spring – super green pea and mint
soup 162
squash *see* butternut squash
Staffordshire oatcakes with roast
balsamic tomatoes and crispy
kale 199
stews
aubergine and chickpea 100
Ethiopian platter 88
sweet potato, cauliflower and
peanut 115
white bean, coconut and roast
pepper 116
Sticky tamarind potatoes 160
Strawberry and peanut butter
crepes 43
Summer in a bowl – panzanella
salad 183
Summer – roast tomato soup
with dill pesto, croutons and
avocado 165
sunflower seeds
dukkah 144
milk 269
and tomato salad 173
sweet potato
and cauliflower and peanut
stew 115
peanut and veg curry 74
sweeteners 16–17

T

tahini 271
   biscuits 239
   coconut cheesecake 214
   coriander dressing 56
   dressing 96, 100, 179
   herby dressing 259
   oats with blackberries 26
Tantalising thali 76
tarts (savoury) heirloom
   tomato 151
tarts (sweet)
   cherry almond 226
   chocolate ganache 224
   lemon and thyme 230
   salted caramel pecan pie 233
thyme
   and butter bean hummus 35
   and cauliflower and butter bean
     soup 166
   crackers 246
   and hazelnut dukkah 252
   and lemon tart 230
toast
   avocado with butter bean and
     thyme hummus 35
   'cheesy' mushrooms and
     spinach 47
   Kim-cheese 36
   Masala beans on toast 32
   peanut butter and banana 38
tofu
   big breakfast shakshuka 55
   and Gado Gado 174
   with greens and fried rice 92
   kimchi gyoza 102
   onion and chickpea frittata 42
tomatoes
   balsamic with baked
     mushrooms 53
   blistered 256
   chutney 86
   confit 264
   and cucumber salad 96
   curry, roast veg and turmeric
     hummus 82

heirloom tart with a walnut
   base 151
and kale with oatcakes 199
marinara sauce 128
multi-coloured salad 173
and pepper sauce 251
and pepper sauce with baked
   mushrooms 108
roasted balsamic with onion and
   chickpea frittata 42
soup with dill pesto 165

U

Ultimate avocado on toast with
   butter bean and thyme
   hummus 35
Ultimate Dijon dressing 260
Ultimate roast veg and chickpea
   tray bake with basil-cashew
   cream 159
Ultimate winter roast lentil and veg
   bake 125

V

vegetables
   big breakfast shakshuka 55
   breakfast curry 63
   caponata 48
   Gado Gado 174
   gobi matar keema 86
   green bean thoran 76
   panzanella salad 183
   roast broccoli with satay
     dressing 154
   roast lentil and veg bake 125
   roast salad with butter beans 179
   roast tray bake with
     chickpeas 159
   roast with tomato curry 82
   shakshuka hummus 244

see also aubergine; beetroot;
   butternut squash; cabbage;
   carrots; cauliflower;
   courgettes; greens; kale;
   mushrooms; onions; peas;
   peppers; potatoes; spinach

W

walnuts
   balsamic and carrot salad 178
   tomato tart 151
Warm roast carrot salad with herby
   lentils and balsamic walnuts 178
White bean, coconut and roast
   pepper stew 116
Winter – lemony spiced lentil and
   chickpea soup with coriander
   dressing 170

Y

yoghurt see coconut yoghurt

About *the* Author

Having started her career in food marketing, Niki created her award-winning blog Rebel Recipes in 2015 after being completely consumed by the food industry. After creating a space to share her easy and accessible plant-based recipes, packed with fresh seasonal organic ingredients, Niki has now worked with numerous household brands developing recipes and creating content for them including Holland and Barrett, Wholefoods, Sainsbury's and Organic UK.

Niki's recipes have been featured in magazines and newspapers across the globe and she regularly coaches, hosts workshops and supper clubs, and appears on panels as an food expert in both the UK and abroad.

Niki is inspiring a new generation of plant-based foodies through her travels and her love and lust for delicious combinations, flavours and techniques.

Niki is a certified Holistic Health Coach and Plantlab Level 1 Raw Chef.

rebelrecipes.com / @rebelrecipes

Acknowledgements

I just want to say a huge thank you to everyone who has made this possible. Those that follow my food adventures; cook my recipes; support and encourage me daily. This book is for you – thank you.

Of course, this wouldn't be possible without my amazing publisher – Absolute and the lovely team (Emily, Marie and Jon) for believing in my recipes and my annoyingly specific layout ideas, which I hope you are enjoying. You are all the best.

Thank you to Kris Kirkham, our super talented photographer and fellow lover of high contrast, rustic shots, for bringing my vision to life and for loving my salted caramel pecan pie!

As well as a huge thank you to everyone who worked on the shoot – which was no easy task. Thank you to the amazing Jennie, Amy, Lauren, Sara, Bettina, Georgie and Alice.

And the biggest thank you to my lovely Andy for always eating my food and telling me it's the best thing I've ever made (every time I make something), and for helping me create and bring Rebel Recipes to life.

I also want to thank Malin for her constant and invaluable help and advice; my agent Becky for her excellent advice and for guiding me through the process perfectly.

I couldn't forget a huge thank you to Melissa Robertson who is undoubtedly one of the smartest, strongest and inspiring ladies I know – and very kindly helped me put my thoughts in order to develop my proposal.

And to all my lovely friends who have put up with my food obsessions and taste-tested many of my recipes (mostly curries and extremely garlicky dips) and to my sister Ems for loving all my desserts – even the experiments which sometimes look like falafels.

Mum, thank you. You're the original, no shit, strong lady who always inspired me to be fiercely independent, taught me how to be able to support myself and strive for my dreams. Also, for giving your strange daughter a food budget as a teenager so she could buy her own food. It sparked my passion, even though that generally meant adding curry paste to everything!

Thank you, Vanessa, for patiently reading my intros and giving me wonderful food advice, all over buttery Chardonnay.

And last but definitely not least my amazing friends and food heroes Sara and Bettina. Sara, your support, creative inspiration and hospitality in providing a bed and furry ginger cat cuddles; Bettina, I genuinely don't think the book would actually be here without you. You introduced me to Becky and persuaded me to keep my options open and never to accept less than I deserved. Thank you. You are amazing.

And finally – Gaya Ceramics. Thank you for supplying some of the most beautiful ceramics I have ever seen.

Publisher
Jon Croft

Commissioning Editor
Meg Boas

Senior Editor
Emily North

Art Director and Designer
Marie O'Shepherd

Junior Designer
Anika Schulze

Production Controller
Laura Brodie

Photographer
Kris Kirkham
kriskirkhamphoto.com

Photographer's Assistant
Eydor Rosso Goncalves

Food Stylists
Niki Webster and
Bettina Campolucci Bordi
Madeleine Cuff
Alice Heather
Georgie Hodgson
Sara Kiyo Popowa
Amy Lanza
Lauren Lovatt
Gail Prevezer
Jennie Vincent

Copyeditor
Kate Wanwimolruk

Home Economist
Elaine Byfield

Proofreader
Margaret Haynes

Indexer
Zoe Ross

BLOOMSBURY ABSOLUTE

Bloomsbury Publishing Plc

50 Bedford Square, London, WC1B 3DP, UK

BLOOMSBURY, BLOOMSBURY ABSOLUTE,
the Diana logo and the Absolute Press logo are
trademarks of Bloomsbury Publishing Plc

First published in Great Britain 2019

A catalogue record for this book is available from
the British Library.

Library of Congress Cataloguing-in-Publication data
has been applied for.

ISBN
HB: 9781472966841
ePub: 978147296683
ePDF: 9781472966827

2 4 6 8 10 9 7 5 3 1

Printed and bound in China by C&C Offset Ltd.

Bloomsbury Publishing Plc makes every effort
to ensure that the papers used in the manufacture
of our books are natural, recyclable products
made from wood grown in well-managed forests.
Our manufacturing processes conform to the
environmental regulations of the country of origin.

To find out more about our authors and books
visit www.bloomsbury.com and sign up for our
newsletters.